the joy

of

PISSING

the joy of

of

PISSING

PROFESSOR JIMMY RIDDLE

NFK

An imprint of Mercier Press
Douglas Village, Cork.

ISBN 978-0-9526410-5-6

ISBN 0-952641-05-4

Illustrations by Brian Hogan

Printed and bound by William Clowes Ltd,
Beccles, Suffolk, England

contents

inter urinam et faecem nascimur

Between piss and shite
are we born to life

about the author

Professor Jimmy Riddle did his first pee by the sea. But it wasn't this which inspired him obtain a PhD in Pissology and set up the world's first College of Pissology in Borris in Ossory (located at Ireland's favourite comfort stop). Yet this memory did stay with him as an occasion that he should for some reason remember.

Growing up bilingually the young Jimmy realised that, unlike when people spoke in Irish, people who spoke in English would become very concerned when talking about pissing. They would mask what they wanted to say with all sorts of figures of speech. Whereas in Irish they would casually use one of the only three words there are for pissing: *mún, steall* and *fual*. Being amused by this he duly jotted the English words down and thus started his research. To date he has collected what he believes to be the entire English language slang for the act of pissing and put in writing for the first time all its uses as a descriptive word. He has amassed a treasure of folkloric tales for the colleges' archive and has presented the best of them here in *The Joy of Pissing*.

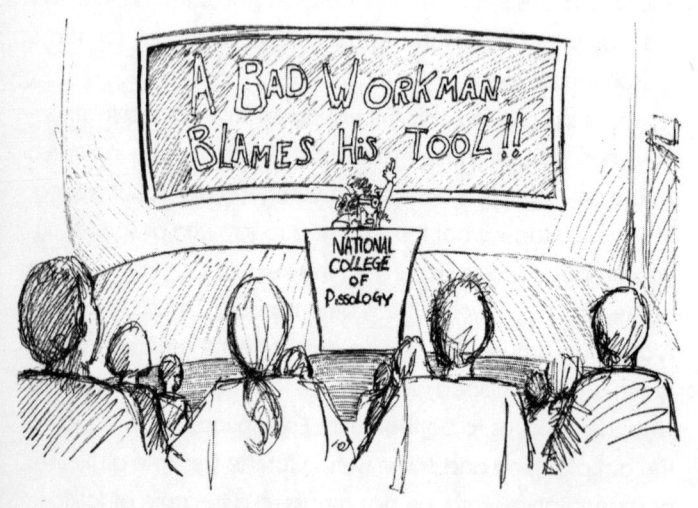

author's note

You are probably wondering how much more you need to know about pissing beyond pointing and flushing. You're probably asking why you should receive any further training for what is, after breathing and eating, the next natural reflex. Like reading, once you've learned, what more does one need to know?

Well, for starters, I don't believe any of us were truly toilet trained. Our parents probably did no more than encourage us to stop soiling our nappies while hurrying us to learn to use the loo. Then, once we could put toilet paper in our hands and flush the cistern the supervision ceased and we were left, forevermore, to our own devices.

The only thing this tuition taught us was to keep our bladders shut until we arrived at a porcelain pot.

Pissing for most people is something that occurs rather than something they take part in. With this book I aim to alter people's urinating habits from something they simply allow to happen to something they will actively participate in.

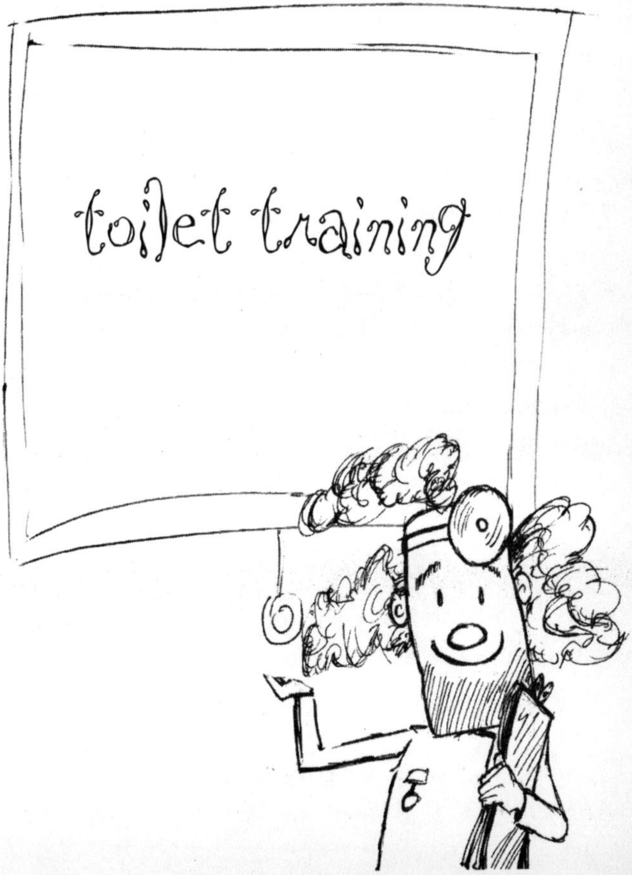
toilet training

Before we do anything we have to agree a few basic rules – the knowledge I am about to impart has taken years of research and practice. Therefore I will appreciate nothing less than your undivided attention. Concentration may only be broken for pee breaks. But only momentarily, because I shall be accompanying you to the loo and it is there that assessment and instruction shall begin in earnest. Now before we begin the first lesson I want you to show me your hands. Hmmm! Did you wash them the last time you used the loo? I thought not. Please go and wash them and return immediately. Now then, are you ready? There's no going back you know. This is an intensive course and I won't be repeating anything. I said I won't be repeating anything. Nothing, no repeats, Ok?, Ok?

how to hold your penis

Ireland's Christian Brothers issued directions on how to pee saying that one must not hold one's penis nor must one make any contact with it when taking it out and putting it back in. If you allow religious values to influence your behaviour, I must pre-warn you that following this advice will lead to innumerable episodes of piddle-stained jocks and dribble-stained robes.

* Of the many methods men have of holding their willies when going for a waz, the most natural and instinctive way is to cup the shaft with all the fingers underneath and the thumb on top. However, due to dribbles and splashes sustained by the fingers, this position is usually abbreviated to just one or two fingers underneath, while the thumb remains on top.

* The next position is the one favoured by dart players. It is the opposite to the above – the thumb goes underneath and just back a bit from the gland. The fingers are placed on top of the penis, and serve to mask the willy from those on the streets or in public toilets wishing to watch.

* Next is the slightly masochistic scissors-holding position. The willy is placed between two fingers, usually with the middle finger underneath and the forefinger on top, as if it's about to be snipped off.

* If you think you have a wild rattlesnake in your trousers, the next holding position is just for you. Place both thumbs on top of the shaft and all eight fingers below (if they fit), thus making sure that no poisonous venom can be sprayed your way.

During the course of my lengthy research I have noted that the right-handed never use the opposite hand when pointing percy at the porcelain whereas left-handers are not so restricted; they can interchange the holding hand at will.

how to stop pissing

Before you start anything you should know how to stop it. If one is to progress to the more advanced stages of pissing, being capable of cutting the flow of one's bladder movements is essential.

Did you ever compete to see how long you could hold your breath as a child? Well we are going to try a similar game only it's a little more difficult and much easier for me to see if you're cheating. So, are you up for the challenge? You're ready that quick? And you really think you'll defeat the champion?

Right then, let's see if you can hold your pee longer than me. On your marks, get set, go! Now, stop the flow! No! Not with your fingers!

Is that it? Is that all you can do? Is that your best effort? Oh! you novices are all the same, always trying to out-do the master as always - 'fools rush in where angels fear to tread'. I just hope you will be as eager to acquire this knowledge as you are to compete.

Right then, put the little lad back in his box and jot down these notes. Here's how it's done. It simply involves tensing the groin muscles and using the tummy muscles to suck the pee back into the bladder. Some women can get quite turned on by practising this, it seems. Either way, this toilet time skill should be practised and practised by all of you, until you are sure you can do it and do it well. Then, and only then, should you contemplate challenging your master.

how to stop Boys from missing the porcelain

A proud mother of three young boys came to me looking for advice after she began noticing big puddles of pee on the bathroom floor by the toilet. Her youngest son was still in nappies, her middle son had just been toilet trained and her eldest son, a teenager, had long ago learned not to piss on the floor.

She feared her youngest son might be trying to copy his brother so when she asked her recently trained son he gave it away by denying it immediately. She cajoled him a bit and then told him that she wouldn't be angry with him if he told the truth and with that he spilled his little his heart out. Innocently he told her that he was trying to clean the grit and grime off the back of the seat by pissing on it.

She praised him for his good intentions but told him that he could do a much better job if used the toilet brush, but to her dismay he didn't care to do that.

She was intrigued when I told her that using their piss jets for target practice was as natural to boys as pissing on a pole was to dogs. For boys, urinating is an active undertaking, whereas for girls it is more of a passive act.

I informed her of a woman I heard on the radio who swore that putting a cork in the loo turned pissing into a sport for the boys in her household. The more effort the boys put into their aim the less stray urine sprays. This meant seat splashes and floor spillages only occurred when the cork sank or had been finally trashed. The universal advice I gave this mother and all mothers with a similar conundrum was to put something in the loo, an apple or a cigarette butt, to give her boys something to aim at.

advanced
pissing skills

how to make Bubbles in the piss Bowl

This is the most basic and perhaps the most important skill the pissing man has had to learn since the creation of the porcelain bowl. You may think it easy to bubble the bowl. Perhaps you feel you're a naturally bubbly individual. Perhaps you're already a long practiced bubble artist who has never registered that you were mastering a valuable skill? However, there is always more to learn.

To begin, you go into the lavatory, you take note of the position of the bowl; tension rises, the spotlight blinks on, a faint drum roll is heard in the distance.

Your thoughts make you hesitate. Will you fail to bubble the bowl? Will you fail due to a lack of juice? Will you fail because you've got too much juice? Never fear. The master is here, help is at hand, and if you sit patiently awhile I shall explain the ins and outs of this difficult but masterable task.

The first obstacle you must overcome is where to start. 'The sides of the bowl? The front? The back?'

No! No! No! None of the above will have the desired effect. Shy pissing is absolutely out of the question, only loud and proud pissers need participate.

You will need to start directly in the centre. Aim your mickey where you think the middle is. Your cock will cock just like a gun so aim a little below where you think the centre is. Begin pissing. Immediately adjust if wrong. A mass of lovely bubbles should begin to form an outward-spreading circle around the jet. If one part is a bit thin on bubbles, angle the jet so as to create more bubbles in that area. Keep peeing for about four seconds, or until there is only a small clear patch in the middle where the jet is connecting with the water. Now grab hold of your shaft to stop the flow. Next, you must use your brain. There is a key question to be answered. How are you going to get all those wonderful bubbles to congregate in the middle? Take note of where the froth is fuller and begin pissing directly into that part.

'No!' I hear you say, 'that will make its own hole which will then have to be incorporated into the rest.'

Yes, yes, I'm glad your grey matter is engaging with the

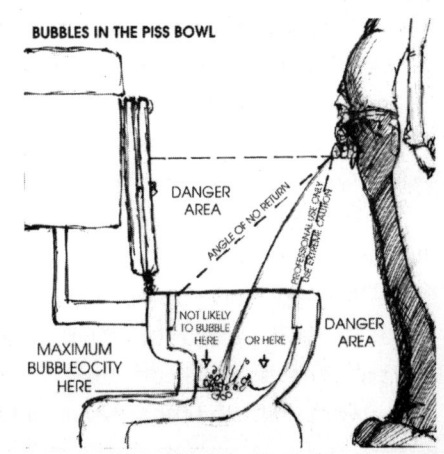

BUBBLES IN THE PISS BOWL

DANGER AREA

ANGLE OF NO RETURN

PROFESSIONAL USE ONLY USE EXHAUST CAUTION

DANGER AREA

NOT LIKELY TO BUBBLE HERE   OR HERE

MAXIMUM BUBBLEOCITY HERE

subject at hand, it's good to see lateral conceptualisers at work. Usually I would frown on non-querying information sponges, but this is a tried and tested method and it works, so listen and learn. You will not make a hole there, because by this stage the froth is quite concentrated, so the more you piddle in it the more bubbles you'll make. Now, if the side you chose is thinning out a bit, aim into the other side. And you've done it. Give yourself a pat on the back – after you've washed your hands.

But what? What did you say? You've still got some more juice left? Ok, don't panic, keep your knickers off. You're afraid that if you pee into the bowl any more you'll spoil the bubbles? Why yes, that would be correct. So hold on to your piss there while you weigh up your options: you could always walk over to the sink and release the rest in there ... but hold on, not so fast, that's cheating and it's really not polite. What you have to do is direct willy marbleside (shy pissing technique) and circulate the urine flow around the inside edge of the bowl until it ceases. This will have the effect of pushing the urine lather away from the side a bit, but, due to a scientific phenomenon called the capillary action (the tendency of solids to attract liquid), the foam will reach back to its ceramic temptress. *Et voilà,* you've done it, a flourish of trumpets should sound in your head. Wash your hands (I know where they've been); stand back quickly to admire your work, and then flush.

Yes, you must! Flushing is a principal part of this practice. This is a kinetic, living artform, and your work of genius is to be admired only by you. I know some of you 'egotesticle' people will want the world to see the bubbled pot and celebrate. But don't be tempted; by the time you grab someone and entice them to admire your exhibition, all of those carefully crafted piss bubbles will have popped back from their rounded H_2O, O, Ur form and returned to their original flat H_2O, Ur form. Besides it is also extremely bad etiquette to leave a bowl of piss for someone else to bubble. So flush, and remember, wash your hands.

Bubble, destroy and reBubblise

So you think you're too skilled a pisser to be spending your precious pissing time in pursuit of professional proficiency in the previous praxis? Well, I bet you can't piss a bowl of bubbles, clear them away and rebubble the whole bowl again.

Well I can, and since I'm such a nice guy I'll share with you my many years of study and practice for this, the pinnacle of the bowl bubbler's craft.

So, you've got all your bubbles there in front of you, but you've still got a full tank. What do you do? No, you don't piss in the sink! Get that idea right out of your head. The sink is exclusively for washing your hands, and I won't be held responsible for any nasty skin disorders that result if you behave like that.

The first step is to hold the flow, and let the top layer of foam clear a bit. Take a moment to enjoy listening to the snap, crackle and pop, then let a bit go and stop again. Repeat this process a few times. What you are now doing is making holes in your earlier work of art. Make about five weak spots in the urine foam, then (and this is important) you go criss-cross, up, down, diagonal, biagonal, triagonal and any other iagonal you can think of. You should have cleared the foam by now. If not, target any last remaining foam deposits and, gently now, destroy!

Ok, the bubbled bowl is not totally clear, but that's pretty good. Now you've a quarter tank left, what do you do with the rest of your bladder juice? No! No! The bath is also for washing yourself. What you do is (say anything else and I'll pull the chair from under your feet) you try to rebubblise the bowl. If you can do that I do believe that you are a deity and need no further teaching from me. I bow in humility, I bend on one knee in obeisance before you. I take your arm and kiss your … ehyuk! For God's sake wash your hands. Jesus! The people I have to put up with.

What? What? What? What do you want now? Oh! Sorry. Your bladder's bursting and you want to know how to rebubblise? Ok! Ok! Hold your horses, let me remember. Hmmmm, right, do you see the bit of foam you didn't clear? Begin pissing there and work your way around the outer side of the bowl. You should now see the bubbles getting bigger in volume, hold the flow one last time, let the urge build, now let your last blast go straight into the middle and Bubbles! Bubbles! Bubbles! Bubbles! Hurray! Beautiful, bountiful bubbles (really big flourish of trumpets heard in background)! Yippee! Bubbles! Bubbles! And more! And more! And more! Bubbles!

fire fighters piss higher

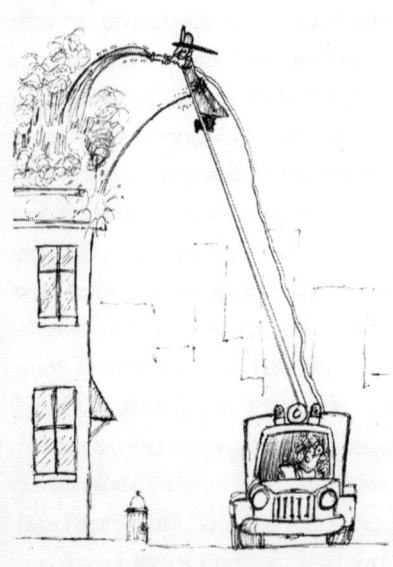

When pissing with friends bubbling is no longer an issue. More important matters like who can piss the highest, the furthest, and the longest take precedence over any of the preliminary skills. Well, they did when I was at school anyway. I have always harboured the notion that one day I might become a fireman from so often being instructed by graffiti written under the roof that 'if you can piss this high you should join the fire brigade'. But if you want to hit the roof with your pee, there is a certain method, which involves a little training.

Sometimes your willy is out and ready to go, but it's, well

let's say, not at its best. To achieve that high-reaching effect, simply pull back your foreskin (if you only have a ring of skin left around your knob after some religious ceremony, pull back whatever you've got). It will have an effect that's something like changing the pressure on a hose. Hold the shaft tight, let the urine build up and then, just as it gets to be too much to hold, let go, simultaneously giving a big pelvic thrust, always aiming upwards. If you can perfect that choreography, you'll soon be taking my place as one of our finest fire fighters.

(Warning: brace the wrist of your foreskin-holding hand against your hip as you thrust, or you may cause painful tearing.)

how to piss with an erection

Of course, none of the previous preparation is necessary if you have an erection. Since erections stand up anyway all you have to do is hold it away from the body a bit (so you don't hit your face), let it build a bit, then off you go, straight up to the higher ranks of the fire brigade.

When not auditioning for a placement in the public service, however, peeing with a boner can be quite tricky, as it is virtually impossible to piss if the erect penis is pushed down perpendicular to the pot. There are only four methods that I am aware of. I'll start with the hardest, which should pose a challenge to the most dextrous of pissers.

METHOD 1:

Firstly, you must judge how strong the initial jet will be, either by using your intuition or by calculating the variable pitch power depending on size of erection, how long after the urge you actually decide to point percy at the porcelain, and other factors such as atmospheric pressure and bowl radius.

When the correct estimate is attained, you must take however many steps are required back, away from the bowl. Unlike a gun, hard-ons tend to lean in one direction, but, like guns, as I already mentioned, they cock slightly upwards when anything is shot through them. (No, that doesn't count as repetition, repeat after me, that doesn't count as repetition.) Many a time I've had to readjust my aim, and clean up after myself. Oh yes, spilling means cleaning, and always lift the seat before pissing, especially before attempting this skill.

So you've begun to piss and you've hit the centre of the water bang on target, when suddenly something goes wrong. The great hose-like feeling you've got begins to diminish, because, as you will notice, the flow gets weaker and your dick gets smaller. You must now begin to retrace the steps you took out, walking back in, and very cautiously at that, making sure you don't overstep and hit the back of the seat, or understep and hit the floor.

You should end up, willy little, finishing your pee above the bowl. Yes, this is a skill that will tax anyone's movement, timing and aiming capabilities. Score eighty-two percent if completed without any outside bowl splashes. And beware an erection often causes a two-tiered pee, but more about that later.

METHOD 2:

All of that is unnecessary though if you have a back wall immediately behind the cistern. This most useful of architectural features can act as a support for your hand as you lean your body at a ninety-degree angle. This position will enable you to hold your erect urinating shaft downwards enough in order to pee into the bowl without having to push it too far down, which as already mentioned, renders the piddle duct impassable by any liquid traffic.

METHOD 3:

If you have no back wall, and are not skilled or confident enough to attempt the first method, there is another way, but unfortunately circumcised males won't be able to do this one as it involves the employment of that useful piece of tissue; the foreskin. If the enlargement of your penis hasn't overstretched the enveloping skin completely, pull what is left of the foreskin over your knob (the gland) and hold the skin as if it was an empty crisp packet you were about to burst. The urine will not flow in ratio to the intensity of your erection, it will trickle and dribble out through the scrunched-up spout you've just created for it. Once your willy decreases in size and you gain more control over the situation you could try bubbling the  bowl, perhaps practise a bit of calligraphy and, as you feel the end arriving, you could pull the chain/press the handle and finish simultaneously with the end of the flush. And if you can do all that during a single performance, believe you me, you're one skilled pisser.

If you must use this technique, be sure to wash your hands and willy afterwards.

METHOD 4:

This method is by far the least taxing and causes the least amount of spillage. Put one foot in front of the pot and bend down on the other knee so that it's resting to the side of the pot; your John Thomas should then be at the same height as the top of the pot. As your pelvis is already slanted you only need slightly tilt percy toward the porcelain. This way pissing with an erection is easy peasy, lemon squeezy.

how to piss off a Bicycle

During a fun-filled six months when our television was on the blink, our family had become very talkative and quite dependent on one another for entertainment. One such night when we were up talking over yet another mug of tea, one of the brothers wobbled in the door looking a bit dishevelled.

He'd had a good few beers and was in one of his chatty moods. Without any prompting he launched into his night's adventures. He began by telling us how he felt too lazy to get off his bike to have a piss, so he took his dick out and just as he was about to pee he crashed into the pavement and fell off his bicycle and found himself on the ground a few moments later still holding his dick. Over the bursts of laughter he said, 'I won't be trying that again, I could've cut me mickey in two.'

The young academic researcher in me was sparked into action that night. Having a mind that won't rest when confronted by an unsolved puzzle such as this, I was charged with a mission to accomplish this highly dangerous feat.

Many's the night-time bike ride home I'd try, but either

the piss would be too shy, or the freewheeling would slow down and re-energising the bike would set back the whole process. Once, some innocent pedestrian saw me preparing for the act. I nearly lost control of the bike and this caused the potential motion to cease up, and no matter how much mental coaxing from my interior mentor, willy wouldn't buy it, and simply refused to pee.

'There must be a way,' I'd tell myself, 'there just must be. Look, you can piss while walking and you've managed to piss while running.' My internal chat would continue, 'you were tempted to try it off a skateboard only the surface was too rough. So what's the big deal with pissing off a moving bicycle?' I'd agree with my mind's coaching, but it would never help me to win the Piss off a Bicycle in Motion Award.

This was the state of affairs until one fateful night, when I was cycling home a wee bit tipsy. I had to pass through a rugby ground with a long stretch of tarmacadam from the clubhouse to the car park, built especially for the likes of me, who want to try out new pissing tricks.

I'd built up a good speed and there was a strong wind behind me. These were the perfect pissing conditions. Feeling the great creative urge several pints can give you, I unzipped my trousers and took d'auld fella out. I straightened my left leg so that I was standing up on the pedal, with my right leg bent on its pedal. I held the handlebars with my right hand and with my left hand aimed my willy under the handlebars and away from the wheel and, lo and behold, I started to piss, without any danger of being caught in the splash zone. What joy I felt that night! What majesty! I had attempted an extremely perilous micturatory task and completed it with first class honours.

I have since done this many times. My longest line of piss was over 200 metres long, I could have gone on longer but I had to stop, because the road I was pissing on, the aptly named, Appian Way, joins with a major thoroughfare into the centre of the city.

PS: a word of warning: Do not to try peeing when freewheel-

Professional cyclists never get off their bikes to micturate. Competition is so rife and seconds lost on the track could mean the difference between a team winning or losing. The cyclist who needs to go gets a team-mate to push him along while he slips it out the side of his tight shorts and dribbles down his legs.

ing down a hill, as fluctuating winds and sudden gusts can blow the pee back onto your clothes and it is very hard to stop fast enough to avoid this.

how to piss into a Bottle

This is quite an important skill. It is not only handy when trying to remain closer to sleep than wakefulness, but it is also useful when you're in confined spaces with no access to a toilet. Most men, on attempting to piss into a bottle, will mistakenly try to fit as much of their penis as possible into the small snout for fear the urine might splash out. The opposite is in fact the case because if you stuff any snout with a spout you create air pressure meaning anything that goes in will shoot straight back out.

In order to piss into a bottle *sans* spillage you must retract your foreskin and only put the very tip of your penis into the bottle mouth, making sure to leave enough space for air to get in and out. This way you will be able to pee into any bottle without fear of leaving a puddle. If you hold the bottle up straight you'll be able to fill it up to the top. When done, screw the cap back on and discreetly dispose of the bottle in any dustbin.

how to piss whilst walking

A feat achieved by pissing to the right when the left foot is taking its step and vice versa. You get this great zig-zag pattern on the pavement and many's the competition I won in my early youth for having done the longest walk whilst pissing (I once won by doing it walking backwards).

how to piss whilst running

A necessary skill most boys learn while running away from their friends who are exploiting a pisser's vulnerability by kicking balls at them or by kicking them in the arse. When in this compromised situation you must strengthen the jet and aim it dead straight ahead and run with your legs wide apart. If your friends get too close your last act of self defence is to simply turn around and spray them with what's left in the bladder. This makes them retreat very quickly.

how to make people piss

We have all gone through a phase of having to change the sheets in the morning, due to bed-wetting dreams. These are not to be confused with wet dreams – or their contemporary, western dreams; when you wake up and you're still shooting. Bed-wetting dreams can occur at any stage after we stop wearing nappies. Even in our teens, twenties or thirties we can find ourselves prone to bed wetting. Those who do may begin to fear they are reverting to a childhood state or have serious doubts about their maturity. But don't worry; half the time it's probably just a friend, brother or sister playing a practical joke on you.

When I was younger, great fun was had watching the dismayed look on a person's face who'd woken up to find a wet patch of urine around their pyjama bottoms. We would wait until the victim was asleep, then run off and get a cup of lukewarm water, take their hand and put it into the cup, and start whispering wonderful watery words while overlaying a generous helping of whish and whoosh sounds for good measure. Within about a minute we could hear, if we could hold back the giggles, the gentle hiss of piss rushing around beneath the blankets. Creased up with laughter we'd fall back into our beds and stay awake that little bit longer in case we were to be the next victim.

In South Korea students who want to retard the urge to piss run a pencil anti-clockwise around the palm of their hand. Whereas when they want to bring on the urge they run it clock-wise round their palm.

how ladies pee and pooh without being heard

Many women muffle splash sounds by employing the toilet paper aided method; stuffing the bowl with loo roll before tinkling. But this cannot be classed as a skill and wastes precious pooh paper. Therefore we will not recommend this practice.

The real skill is in the sitting position. You must sit very close to the front of the bowl, so that your pee won't go anywhere near the water. If you're not comfortable sitting in that position you must learn to propel and aim your piss with the use of certain muscle group somewhere on the ground floor of the department store. This is a bit ambiguous, I know, but my source for this information wouldn't elaborate on the details, and this isn't an anatomy book, yet.

The skill of shitting without a sound was mastered by a student of mine. She explained how she would flush the cistern before the stool could hit the water's surface to avoid that dreaded undignified sound. She also had a swift hand and would have wiped bum and miraculously disposed of the paper before the flush had finished.

Her toilet performances must have all been 'one-shit wonders', never releasing the others for fear they might plop.

The intricacies of this skill are mind-boggling, and before endeavouring to try it out one must first know how much was to be crapped, then, one would need to calculate the speed of drop by taking into consideration the height above the water and the gravitational pull, then you would need to accurately assume how fast the flush would fall and how long it would last, in order to wipe your bum well and dispose of the paper during the final stages of the flush.

And all because the lady loathed loud loos.

How not to make a noiseless piss:
A mature student told how on the night of his honeymoon he was so afraid of being heard pissing by his wife that he put his foot into the bowl and pissed down his leg!

how women can pee standing up

Not being able to pee standing up without taking off their pants has been a source of annoyance and envy for women since the beginning of time. The joy of being able to pee freely in an upright position has eluded women for too long. We are the only mammals on this earth who enjoy bipedal movement. It therefore follows that both sexes should benefit from straight-legged bladder relief. There are many methods and all one need do is practise a little. Urethral sphincter muscle and pelvic floor (the department store ground floor) exercises will vastly improve your ability to carry out these skills. So get squeezing. The best way to begin your practice is in the shower. If you do piss in the shower, why not make this practice a productive one?

THE FINGER-AIDED METHOD:

As a long-serving professor, I appreciate that women would be less keen to take detailed anatomical pissing lessons from a male practitioner. So I will hand you over to my assertive, yet learned, female assistant Ms Jenny Riddle who, I believe, is more capable in this field than I. Those intending to take part in Jenny Riddle's class should make their way up the hall and go into the shower room on the left.

Afternoon sisters! My name is Ms Riddle, we have a lot to learn and a short time in which to learn it. Squeamish-ness won't be tolerated, if we want to piss like men we have to think and talk like men. So I'm not going to beat around the bush.

Right then, off with the clothes, towels ready, get your bladders ready to piss and piss holes ready to learn.

Are we all paying attention? Step into the shower, they should be warm by now. Stand up straight, spread your legs, place your middle and fore fingers between your lips and spread 'em. The correct place to rest your

41

fingers is just above your pee hole, do not place them either side, as this will distort the angle of the jet. Right then, let's get pissing!

Now, if you are pissing in a straight line downwards this is good, but we want to piss out from our bodies. To do this pull your fanny up toward your belly button so that you are pissing at a spot twelve inches away from you (US students note: fanny means vagina, not your bottom). Pulling up too high will cause you to spray; so easy on those lips, ladies.

If you are peeing down your leg, this is because you are applying too much pressure to one side of your labia. The whole key to success is knowing exactly where to put your fingers. It's like learning to whistle; you have to know how to position your lips to achieve the best results. Ok! Finish up, grab a towel, and drink some dandelion tea; this should get your bladder going again in a few minutes.

When we resume the lesson, we'll be practising accuracy. As 'seat splash' sufferers we know that most men have yet to master the skill of accuracy. If we are going to pee standing up, we are going to do it better than men. We won't leave splashes on the seat like them.

This lesson is not about being able to pee like men; it's about learning to pee like women.

Finish your tea and get back into your showers! Turn on the water and get yourselves nice and warm. We want to focus our minds and think of a straight line. Right! Turn off the water, take this standard size paint pot and place it on the shower floor in front of you. You are going to follow the previous procedures only this time you will aim your piss into the pot. The better you get the further you should move the pot away. Over the next hour the pots are going to get smaller and smaller and once we have achieved optimum accuracy we will take away the pots and you will be aiming directly into the drain. So we want to concentrate sisters, concentrate.

Ok! Let's get pissing. If for some anatomical reason your pee is veering off to one side you'll need to compensate by gently pulling one of the piss flaps slightly to get the stream to go straight. If the stream is going in the left direction, you should pull slightly on the left piss flap. Some of you lucky devils may have a naturally forward pointing urethra, which will mean you won't have to use your hands at all, but the rest of us mere mortals will just have to follow the above steps.

Ok so, how are we doing ladies? I see some of you have achieved pin-point accuracy. When you go home I want you to try pissing out straight. You have the technique and the skill. All you need now is the will. Ok! Thank you for your attention sisters, your class is over now. You can turn the shower back on, clean up and finish off. Fresh towels will be provided on request.

Most of you by this stage will know if you will be able to master this skill or not. If you can, you must make it your purpose from now on to stand every time you need to pee. That means no more passive pissing! You are no longer women; you are training to become womyn. For those of you who may not be able to cope with the level of self discipline required to master this act there is still hope. Mr Riddle will be handing out leaflets on the many devices that can help us to piss standing up.

PISSING UPRIGHT IN PUBLIC

For those of you who dislike the vulnerable, undignified feeling of crouching behind cars while your friends keep watch, but have not mastered how to pee out through the zip of your jeans with your trousers still fastened to your waist, here are a few stand-up methods you may find useful.

If you're wearing pants there are two methods of peeing up against a wall without having to drop your trousers around your ankles.

Bum to the wall: Bring your trousers half-way down your thigh. Bend the knees and bend your body over a bit so that your pee spot is pointing toward the wall, take aim and shoot. You will have the advantage of facing out. That way you can keep watch for people, but pulling up your jeans in this position may expose your pubic region for a millisecond longer than you would wish.

Front bum to the wall: Face the wall, jeans to half thigh, fingers separating labia, drag skin upward, bend back, push hips forward, point and shoot. This method may expose your posterior but then again the milli-metre of fibre that comes between a

45

woman's bottom and a man's gaze doesn't really hide anything anyway.

If you are into wearing long skirts and no underwear it is easy to water the flowers standing up. You need only spread your legs and pull the skirt out in front of you. Learning not to spray your legs or material is the hard bit but after only one lesson with Ms Riddle you should be able to master it.

PEEING STANDING UP WITH THE AID OF DEVICES

We in the College of Pissology highly recommend these inventions. Now women can piss their names in the snow, just like their younger brothers do.

* **Travel Mate** is the best of all and won a medical design award in 2001. It resembles a Kazoo but with a biologically designed catchment area that is to be placed between the lips and directly under the pee spot. You won't need toilet paper because the Travel Mate wipes off residual urine.

  It's reusable and it floats, meaning that if you drop it over a boat you can retrieve it. Accessories, like hygiene sprays to keep the funnel clean, and discreet leather or velvet carry cases can also be bought to make the experience even more formal.

* **The Freshette** is a palm-sized, portable restroom designed especially for women who take long car rides or for times when sanitary facilities are unavailable. The kit contains a discreet 'fleshtone' unit, clear bevelled extension, a 'readycase', and 12 disposable bags, all in a zippered carry pouch.

* **The Lady J** is a concave, diamond-shaped implement with a small nozzle at the front, designed to cover the entire area of the vagina meaning there is absolutely no chance of spillage. Those who have a problem with longer nozzles being too penile will be happy with this.

* **Semi-cone** is the cheapest device available. It resembles a paper popcorn cone, cut in half, lengthways. It is wax covered and can be held below the vagina to act as a funnel to ferry fluids forth. Irish music festivals and Italian petrol stations already sell these.

* **The Riddlette** is custom designed by Professor Riddle to fit all fannies, with a simulated foreskin pressure gauge and made from self-cleansing industrial grade polyfibres. Although it is the most expensive on the market it is also the most useful.

urinals in the ladies': no longer will ladies need to queue for the loo

We have been toying with the idea of putting urinals in the ladies' toilets in the college but the Union of Female Students have not come to an agreement on that issue yet. The more vocal students don't think they will be successful until the design allows women to maintain their privacy and also not have to worry about coming into contact with unsanitary surfaces. We in the college staff room have discussed whether femaie urinals would catch on, what with the inability to use them for anything else. But it has been noted that there are enough girls of strong character out there who would have no compunction about going for a pee in front of complete strangers.

48

You may not believe this but it was back in the 1950s when the first female urinals were mass-produced and installed in public toilets in the US. They were wall mounted and in the shape of a keyhole. Legs would straddle the thin part and bottoms would hover over the round part. They probably went out of favour when women started wearing trousers, because prior to that skirts would have afforded women some cover.

The Lady Loo is the first female urinal of its kind in Asia and since Malaysia's largest shopping mall has already installed them it seems likely that they will go into mass production. They have a built-in bidet, which eliminates the use of a hand-held nozzle and they also come with an automatic flush system.

So is it time for women to stand up and bubble the bowl like men?

the finer
piss arts

piss artists

Let's say you've become tired of bubblising and want to channel your creative impulses toward a more natural method of expression – one entirely organic and full of primal vigour, yet possessed of its own mysterious integrity. If you feel this, then it sounds like the discipline of piss art is for you.

'Piss artist' used as a term of abuse is a misuse of the English language. The very word artist suggests a skilled person, one who has undergone some form of training and can, in some way, express things that could not properly be expressed through the medium of speech. You will often hear conversations like this:

> *Yer man there on the drums, he's not really all that good, is he?*
> *Yer right there, he's a fucking piss artist.*

> *What d'ye think of Jockser, he was a bit funny with me last night?*
> *Don't mind him, he's nuttin' bur ah piss artist.*

However, true piss artists, like pop artists, must undergo years of rigorous training to hone their skills to a high level of consistency. Piss artists have much the same ideals as pop artists: to make high art out of low culture. Whereas pop artists used Campbell's soup cans to express society's dire need for artistic literacy, piss artists use no more than their natural apparatus to express a dire need for a pee.

Pavement piss prints, like popular art forms, are transient: you pass water, it passes into thin air. Therefore, it is hard to achieve any great level of distinction or notoriety in this game. There are, however, those who have used certain methods to record their efforts and they have somehow made the leap from living art to permanent art. For instance, there is a famous anecdote which tells the tale of Jackson Pollock pissing into Peggy Guggenheim's fireplace. All the guests thought this was just another expression of his art.

* **Photographically:** In 1961 Andy Warhol did his first urination paintings but only a photograph remains.

* **Chemically:** During the 1970s Warhol went one step further and immortalised his and his friends' piss by pissing on to canvasses prepared with copper paint. The ensuing patterns that evolved were called the oxidation paintings.

* **In colour:** In 1918 Tristan Tzara proclaimed in the Dadaist Manifesto that everyone has 'the right to piss in different colours'. Fifty years later, three thousand people paid 3Fr each to view an exhibition entitled 'The Void' by Yves Klein. They were each served a cocktail and brought to a room with nothing but blank white walls. The people cried foul and the police were called. The next morning all those who drank the cocktail went to the loo and pissed in blue. And that's pure true.

* **Recorded sound:** In 1991 Tom Marioni, founder of the Museum of Conceptual Art in San Francisco, produced a 'soundwork' by recording himself urinating, and called it 'The Yellow Sound, for Kandinsky'.

* **In Plaster:** The conceptual artist Helen Chadwick, when offered an artist-in-residence stint in the town of Banff in

the Canadian Rockies, decided to make plastercasts of her own and male friend Dave's simultaneous piss indentations in the snow. She called them piss flowers.

Helen mistakenly categorised her flowers as erotic art. They are in fact piss art. So, when in Canada, 'Watch where the huskies go, and don't you eat that yellow snow' (as all Eskimos know).

As the finest piss artist alive, I, in all my professorship, believe that recording the event goes against the essential purity of this art form. Piss art is live art; your drawing space is limit-less, you need purchase nothing ... well, maybe a few pints (though I doubt you'll get a grant for that). What and where you piss is your exhibition space; it is instant and will last about five minutes at most, and then your work will evaporate to make way for the next passing piss artist.

how to Become a piss artist

To attain the mastery of craft and technique that a prac-tising piss artist such as Max Liebermann has achieved, you must start your training back at base – at the bowl.

Every artist has humble beginnings. So this is how to begin: unzip, unbutton or untie your trousers to release the jailbird, take him in hand, and begin to piss. Now, try to draw the letter 'O' (that's an easy one, you've done that during the first phase of bowl bubbling). Just go around in a circle. No! Don't walk around in a circle, you dimwit (you're cleaning that up, by the way). I meant encircle your piss. OK! Next! This one is a little harder. Write the letter 'P'. If you are right-handed you will probably write P with three strokes: down, back up and around.

Yep, just as I thought. Right-handers, you must unlearn this habit, you are wasting precious ink. You must draw it like those thrifty left-handers in two strokes (start from the bottom, and just go up and around. Ahh, very good, very good, that makes sense, doesn't it?) Just practise those two until you're finished, then flush and wash your hands.

Max Lieberman, a German painter and etcher who specialised in genre scenes and portraits, derided a fellow artist who was having difficulty draw-ing General Paul Von Hindenburg's face with the quip; 'I could piss the old boy in snow.'

Next time you go, try all the letters in the alphabet (if you can last the pace that is). Always keep in mind the 'conserve your piss' principle. Letters like D, B, R and P, that usually take three movements, can be done with two instead. For any other letter that has an unnecessary pee-stroke, just cut that stroke out. What must be done to avoid letters like T, F and K looking messy is draw the first stroke of the letter, hold the flow, reposition, and then do the second. Finish, flush, hand wash.

The next time you need to go I want you to try writing your name. Don't worry yourself with self-defeating thoughts like, 'Am I pissing on my name?' You are not. You are pissing your name, which is subtly but fundamentally different and has no negative metaphoric connotations. One of the perks of this practice is that you might (I did anyway) get a visual impression of your name in three dimensions, crossing over the back of your retina from left to right, or you may visualise your name slowly morphing into itself, or… Oh! Sorry, I mustn't deny you your own imagination. Fetch me my cane so I may re-beat that lesson back onto my back.

The next step is a big one. You are going to take your skills out onto the streets, where they can be publicly appreciated. Oh, but you're thinking 'I haven't got the balls'. Bollocks! What's in that sac dangling between your legs, huh?

And anyway, how many times have you gone for a few pints and on leaving the pub, bursting to go, have said, 'Hang on lads while I take a leak'? Then off you've gone to some nearby lamppost or shop entrance for a slash and if anyone should bother you you'd offer, 'a man's gotta do what a man's gotta do.' Well, all you have to do now is defend your dignity with a similar sentiment: 'a man's gotta draw what a man's gotta draw.'

Don't be swayed by the public's distasteful reactions to your exhibition piece. Every artist's first attempts are criticised. At its worst your first effort might vaguely resemble a bad silhouette of a skyward-shooting fountain in the wind, which is quite funny all the same. However, with all the practice you are about to do, you'll do better than that, I know you will. You'll be able to write such silly things as 'watch your step', 'I was here ' or 'elephant' (the latter always confuses people). You could start drawing matchstick men and keep practising until you eventually arrive at the point where you could piss Max Liebermann's own face in the snow. Then and only then will you be a true master piss artist. But really, being a piss artist in training is much more fun.

pissing competitions

HOW MANY Ss CAN YOU ADD TO PISSSSSSSSSS?

A new competition will soon be sweeping the nation (so mind where you walk, fellow earthlings): the adding of as many extra Ss to the word PISS. As I'm the only person currently practising this skill (my brothers and sisters you disappoint me), I must still boast of holding the world record of thirty-two Ss. I achieved this amazing feat of stamina outside the Bleeding Horse, a pub in Dublin. My previous record was fourteen, and it was seven before that, so I must have been haemorrhaging. And no, I wasn't seeing double, I have a witness to prove it. Here's how it was achieved: I was on my fourth pint and hadn't yet visited the loo. Bladder aching and knees wobbling, I got up and excused myself with the traditional, 'excuse me, ladies, while I powder my prick'. The stairs being too difficult to climb added to the overwhelming urge for some great creative expression and, seeing as I prefer pissing outdoors anyway, I decided to perfom outside. Seeing a large area of vacant, pristine cement outside, I couldn't resist the temptation and so I began to PISSSSSSS. Hordes of people passed by, pointing at me and laughing, but I refused to be distracted. The task demands intense concentration. Even in my drunken state my well-honed skills did not abandon me.

I can see it now; in the years after I am dead they will be celebrating me like Joyce. Instead of 'Bloomsday' people will celebrate 'Riddlesday'. Pilgrims will visit and piss in the many spots around the city I have pissed in. My pissing will immortalise me. Some men are known for their excellence and I shall be known for the pisssss on the pavements.

I must have been gone quite a while, because a friend came out looking for me. He found me counting out loud. 'Jimmy,' he said, 'what are you doing? Come on we're all going.' I greeted him with a footballer's hug and screamed in his ear, 'Thirty-two! Look, thirty-two! Come here, I'll count it out for you!' He didn't seem to understand the momentousness of the occasion. He just said, 'Look Jimmy, you're pissed, let's go.'

I went straight into 'A dhaoine uaisle agus ísle, hic, I graciously accept this award on behalf of the police who never caught me. Hic, it has always been my philosophy that the world is your urinal, hic, so never miss a chance to piss. The piss artist's motto, Hic, iss "The wall is my display; I'll piss on it what I may". On a nighse like this ...'

'Jimmy!' my friend burst in, 'what are you shittin' on about? Will ye shut up!'

the perpetual pee

During my years of research I came upon this fact; the longest lasting piss ever recorded went on for twenty-four minutes. There was no mention of how it was achieved so I searched *The Guinness Book of Records* but they don't report these incidents for fear they might encourage them. Therefore I propose we publish *The Jimmy Riddle Book of Records* for all the stranger human achievements.

I have often wondered what rules would regulate such a competition and what technique the record holder used to win; did he hold his piss for a couple of days beforehand and blast away on competition day? Or did he just let a couple of dribbles out every minute or so, holding it in for the rest of the time? Or was it a constant but very slow dribble?

Further into my theorising I concluded that if the record-holder were allowed to drink before and during the competition, he could actually achieve a perpetual pee; Assuming it takes half an hour to digest a half pint of beer, we can safely assume it takes the same time for water to pass through you. So, if you were to drink a pint of water a half-hour before

'hold it, hold it, on your marks...'

pissing and keep taking large gulps from thereon, you could surely achieve the pisser's holy grail. This is similar to the principle of 'circular breathing', whereby a didgeridoo player can inhale through his nose while exhaling through his mouth *ad infinitum*.

Being the most skilled pisser in the world, and pretty handy on the didgeridoo, I reckon I should easily be able to blast away that twenty-four-minute record.

So Jimmy Riddles own records so far are as follows:

* Longest piss from bike: 200 metres not out.

* Longest piss from vehicle: 3 miles long.

* Longest piss from stationary position: 1.5 minutes with no breaks.
* Longest length of piss from height: 33 feet.

the longest length of piss

My longest length of piss was 33 feet. Not bad I hear you say but I can hear you all musing to yourselves, I pissed from a height higher than that, I pissed off the Eiffel Tower or I pissed off the Empire State, or I pissed off the stands onto the football supporters below. Yes, yes, very good, you may have done so, but you didn't do it sitting down, nor do you play the didgeridoo, which I do. Ahem!

There I was, in a friend's flat bursting for a piss after drinking a load of tea. I was reluctant leave the room because that would disrupt the convivial atmosphere and break the momentum and flow of our conversation. So, says I, 'Here, can I piss out your window?'

'Ah Jaysus,' replied my friend, with the pain of coercion showing plainly on his face.

'Don't worry, I won't piss inside,' I assured him. The window was the modern PVC type that doesn't open upward, only inward from the bottom, and it was tricky to squeeze through.

'Ah Jaysus, Jimmy,' my friend moaned.

I got out onto the ledge, sat down, took out me diddler and, with one hand inside the window holding on and the other directing the flow of things, I began to pee. I was amazed – my pee took about two seconds to drop, and it hit the concrete below with a beautiful, resonant splatter echoing musically between the walls of the neighbour's house and the house from which I was pissing. I would happily have stayed in that moment forever.

My friend was constantly on my case, urging me to stop for fear I'd wake the neighbours, but it was just too good to stop. When I came back in we both cracked up laughing for a good ten minutes, so much so that my friend had to go to the toilet himself. Not being brave enough to try it off the window ledge, he went downstairs to the toilet, thereby breaking the atmosphere that had induced me to piss off the ledge in the first place.

Who can piss the highest

There is a story circulating in the college at the moment about a group of dedicated students who were discussing the concept of male physical superiority. The girls wouldn't accept that their anatomy was inferior to that of the guys so the men asked them to name one thing that women could do better than men. One of the girls said that women could piss higher. After much debating there was nothing for it but to organise a competition. It was agreed that the losing sex would have to buy drinks for the rest of the night.

They all gathered around in the back yard, and two contestants of equal height stood at the wall – she with her pants down and her ass to the wall and he facing the wall with his willy in hand. Before they began she looked up and noticing this she said, 'Hey! No hands! You don't see me using any.' Unable to come up with any reasonable excuse as to why he should be allowed to he had to accept this condition.

Then the pissing and the cheering began. After much backward and forward pelvic thrusts from both contestants accompanied by roars of laughter from their supporters, the pissing ended. The measuring tape wasn't needed as it was

Patrick Kavanagh, the writer, in his weekly column *A Countryman's Diary* fondly recounted how he used to take part in a high pissing competition against the gable wall of the church in Inis Keen in County Monaghan.

plain to see that the female student was far superior than the guy. Feminine physicality had won and the men just stood back, amazed. The winner later revealed that she was Ms Jenny Riddle's best student.

Who can piss the furthest

Ms Jenny Riddle's mother told her how she once challenged a group of young boys and elderly men who used to piss off the local bridge every Sunday after mass. She decided to try to put an end to their bad behaviour by challenging them to a pissing contest. If she won they'd have to stop their play, and if she lost she vowed to clean out each of their cow-sheds on a weekly basis.

So a date was set; after mass the next Sunday the pissing would begin. No one paid any attention to the sermon that Sunday as all the villagers' minds were focused on the event ahead. Much to the surprise of the priest, no one stayed around the church after the service. Intrigued by this, he went out to see where everyone had gone. From the church door he spotted two people standing on the edge of the bridge with one of them in what seemed to be a dress. He also noticed a bigger crowd than that which had attended mass gathered around them. The dress was lifted and a great big cheer exploded from the crowd marking the start of the contest.

Horrified at what was taking place the priest ran to the bridge to try and stop such unchristian behaviour. But respected as he was they wouldn't let him through. The end of the competition and the winner was signalled by the overexcited shrieks from the women and the sighs from the men. Being the more masterful at the task, the lady won, and the men arrested their weekly post-praying practice forever. It was the priest, however, who took all the credit for this. At

mass the next week he blasted the church goers with threats of hell and damnation should such a thing happen within the sight of the house of God again, and he vowed a harsh penance in confession for those who carried out the deed. Needless to say no one owned up.

Who can piss the most?

Drunkenness makes people do all sorts of silly things. Students from our 'pissing in a space capsule' research department were having a wine tasting evening. They were taught all about consistency, nose, tannins of different wines. But the tasting turned into a drinking competition and then got quite out of hand when someone suggested they have a pissing competition. 'Let's see who can piss the most after half an hour's drinking!' With that they downed as much wine as they could. When the time was up they all lined up and in front of each other, male and female, student and tutor, all competing to win a case full of Gran Reserva. Students mocked each other's efforts for having a 'bad nose', 'being too cloudy' or and 'lacking in vigour' as they filled glass after glass. In the end a female student won but her glory was diminished as the janitor threatened to report her if she didn't clean up the next day.

tales of
urination

pissing in a taxi

A taxi man ranted this story at me when I asked him whether it was true that they had a soiling charge.

'Women are the worst', he told me, 'they come out of the pubs, full of drink, the cold shrinks their bladders, but instead of peeing in the street, they head straight for the taxi rank where they might stand bladders bursting for an hour or two. All they have to say is "hold me place, I'll be back in a minute", but no, they'll never leave to take a leak because they don't trust the others in the queue.'

'It's the heating that makes them do it,' he said, 'once they get in to a warm environment all their muscles relax. They may try to stop themselves but holding that much in for over an hour is too much for them to bear.'

He told me about the night he was dropping a less than sober, well-to-do woman off at her house. As she was getting out of the car he looked over to see if she was leaving anything behind when he saw steam rising from her leg. He didn't twig what was going on until he focused his gaze closer. Shocked at what he was seeing he yelled, 'What the fuck do you think you're doing? Get out! Get out! Stop pissing in me car.' Realising she had been caught, she apologised profusely and explained how she didn't want to run out of the car and into her house for fear he'd think she didn't want to pay.

'But why didn't you ask me to stop along the way?'

'I couldn't, I'd be scarlet.'

'But you're not embarrassed about pissing in my car?'

'Oh look, I'm really sorry mister but ye know the way it is.'

Not feeling any sense of pity he said, 'you've wrecked me night's earnin's now, look the seat and the floor's covered in it, I can't get another fare until it's cleaned up.' She offered him double the money but he took the charge sheet off the dash and pointed out the €70 soiling charge.

'And they give out to us for pissin' in the street.'

holy water

I was sitting in a room with a bunch of colleagues during a boring rugby playoff for the wooden spoon, when one of the girls started to recount with great enthusiasm the previous night's adventure. On the mention of the ladies' toilet, all male ears pricked up, the zapper was reached for and as the volume was being lowered she was told to halt her tale.

She said she'd been drinking in one of Dublin's tiny watering holes, which has a tiny hole in which to water as one of

its classic features. On feeling the diuretic effect of her beer consumption, she walked into the ladies' loo, and was greeted by the usual queue of holes waiting to water. Seeing as she was fifth in the queue and the only two cubicles were in use, she said out loud, 'Listen girls, the sink is free, whether it's holy or not I'm going to water this hole.'

None of the girls seemed surprised, as they had exactly the same thing in mind, but before she could undo her belt buckle the girl at the top of the queue turned around and warned her with a cautionary tale. A friend of hers, who could not find a place to pee during the latter stages of a house party, decided in her desperation to piss in the kitchen sink. She got up on the sink and the next thing she remembered was being woken by her boyfriend's parents, soaking wet, knickers around her ankles, water gushing everywhere and the aluminium sink collapsed on the ground.

Judging by the size of the toilet sink, and how much more sturdy an aluminium kitchen sink would be in comparison, she thought it wiser to hold her water.

When she finally got into the latrine and was letting her water to hole, she heard the entrance door slam open and a drunk girl, with a less than watertight hole, ordering the patiently waiting queue out of her way. Moments later there was a loud crash and some terrified gasps and yelps, which made those in the cubicles put their water on hold. Unable to piddle any more, our friend pulled up her trousers, flushed and rushed to the rescue, only to see an overweight girl being lifted up off the ground and another girl trying to reconnect the miniature sink back to the wall. They all looked at each other and burst their holes laughing.

One of the guys who had been watching the match quickly added, 'So you can bring your hole to water, but the altar must be built to hold.'

the toilet tamer

We often stand naked in front of some of the most dangerous white monsters in the world. We, the brave, sit on their lips and shit in their mouths, arrogantly presuming that they'll swallow the lot. This is not always the case. Sometimes, when we least expect it, the beast will awaken, mad with rage, and violently spit the full amount back out with a shite for a shite and a stool for a stool Biblical vengeance.

One fine day, there I was in a cubicle, just finished with both orifice one and orifice two, bum hygienically wiped. I'd thrown the last bit of tissue into the toilet and flushed it. I was just about to reach down to pull up my trousers when I saw the water level rising. I'd woken the beast, what would I do now? Normally I'd lash out a few cracks of my whip, bought especially for this purpose, and the fiend would retreat. But today the whip was at home and I was in college, in a very small toilet cubicle with a door that opened inwards, my trousers around my ankles and the water level rising and rising. I couldn't jump up on to the bowl and thus escape over the wall because firstly I'd have to reach down to pull up my trousers, and then I'd get my long hair wet. The water level kept rising. I'd have to think fast. To open the door I'd have to stand behind the bowl but being unable to pull up my trousers I would be exposing myself with my trousers down to those outside. The water rose to the top and I stood motionless in the corner of the cubicle, balls hanging out, in a total stalemate.

I stood awaiting the onslaught: soaked shoes, socks and trousers, my own effluent passing under the door and out all over the tiles in the washing area. For a college professor this would be very unseemly. When suddenly something – a kind spirit? My guardian angel? To this day I don't know – pacified the toilet's rage and it began to retreat, back to whence it came. As I watched the water sink back down the sewer pipe I was afraid even to breathe, lest 'Loocifer' would rise again. He didn't. I counted my blessings and bowed in thankfulness to whatever it was that saved me.

But what was it that awoke the beast? Was it mad at my offerings? Was there too little or too much? Possibly the wrong kind of stuff? Not enough fibre perhaps? I pulled up my trousers and got out of there fast.

sporting piddlers

I was exchanging stories about youthful sporting days as Gaelic footballers with a bunch of mates over a few pints. These are some of the stories that came up.

Speedy told us how it was he was so fast. The powerful urge to urinate during a match used to keep him running around for fear he couldn't contain it if he stopped. But, he admitted, by half time he'd be completely knackered.

'You couldn't just leave the pitch,' he reasoned, as match and club suspension would surely result.

Feisty, the full forward, used to play for such a crap team that an opposing goalie once decided he had enough time to take out his diddler and piddle up against the post.

A referee, we were told, once stopped a match after fifteen minutes to relieve himself against a nearby tree.

Then, Badger the Bogger told us about his old Westmeath team who were so dedicated (to their drink) that they'd have to be dragged from their beds and topped up with painkillers to cure their heads from the previous night's piss-up. On one occasion, due to a lack of players, the manager had to play himself. About five minutes after the ball was thrown in, to the bafflement of the two teams, the ref blew his whistle. The playing stopped and the players all looked toward the ref, who was frantically waving a red card and running toward the sideline. The player manager was in a crouched position just off the pitch, evacuating his bladder and bowels on the grass. Being so eager that morning to get his team together, he had forgotten to go to the loo.

Padjo told us how, back in the 1950s, his dad's team used to play on a pitch where cows grazed and would only be cleared away shortly before a match. The opposing team would cower away from tackles, for fear of falling face first into the multitude of cowpats decorating the pitch. Our friend's father's team would smear the ball with cowshit before taking free kicks, forty-fives or goal kicks so only the bravest from the other team would ever try to catch the ball, so inevitably the home team would always win. Then, unhindered by the fact that they had no washing facilities, off to the local *céilí* they'd go with the scent of warm animal musk as their only BO-dorant.

sleepwalking piddlers

We have discussed this phenomenon at length in between lectures and I've heard nightmare stories from sleepwalkers who after a heavy night's drinking were found pissing into cupboards, flowerpots, the oven, and one, all over the clothes on a neighbour's washing line. I have concluded that incidents such as these are universal, and will occur whenever there's a sleepwalker and drink in the same bed.

A university dean told how, as a teenager, he was so intoxicated that he had to be carried to his bed. Not long after, he was seen by his mother dancing around his room, willy in hand, pissing all over the carpet. When he complained the next morning that someone had poured a bucket of water all over in his room, his mother chided him for being so insolent and treated him to a long lecture on the evils of drink. She had apparently tried to wake him up but, he had turned his jet stream at her and chased her out of the room.

A visiting lecturer told how he was woken up by his flatmate one night, only to find he was standing above his him, dick in hand, ready to piss on his frightened friend's face.

But worst of all was the second-year student who, after a manic drinking party in his friend's house, somehow managed to go upstairs, undress and crawl into bed. He had a rude awakening: an almighty slap in the face, followed by some unbearable shrieking and screeching. His friend's mother was screaming at him, 'You dirty filthy pig! You're pissing in my bed!! How dare you! How dare you get into my bed – naked! And how dare you piss in it! Get out! Get out!! GET OUT!!!'

damn the dick
or take the
stick

Danger foreshadows
Those who don't know
How to stem the flow.

delivery Boy

I was dared once to piss into a letterbox by my giddy teenage friends. This dare fed right into the revenge fantasies I had as a paper delivery boy, so I decided to accept the challenge. I opened the gate to this old Georgian house, walked up the steps to the large wooden front door, took my willy out, got up on my tippy-toes, pushed open the tightly-sprung brass letterbox flap, stuck my willy in and started to pee. In knots of laughter I turned my head to share the joke with my mates, only to be greeted by the blank stare of a policeman's face. You can imagine the terror I felt – I nearly chopped my dick in two letting go of letterbox flap. Not knowing how to cut my flow I stuffed my dick back into my trousers and ran down the steps and out the gate. I ran across the road to where my friends were. Amazingly, the policeman didn't notice what was going on – I suppose his job description didn't require that he be on the lookout for young louts pissing in people's post boxes. He must have thought I was innocently delivering a letter. Delivering a baby more like it!

urine sample

When coming out of anaesthesia in hospital once, I heard the sound of a nurse pulling across the curtains to conceal me from the rest of the ward. That done, she said, 'Mr Riddle, we would like a urine sample', and handed me a stainless-steel container, covered by a white paper bag.

I was so weak, I could hardly sit up. Container in hand, ready to unleash me diddler, I noticed something strange out of the corner of my eye – the nurse was still standing there. I looked up at her to see what her trip was. Nothing, no response, not even a blink. She was as disinterested as a queen receiving food from a servant. I looked down to take stock of the situation, then looking back up at her I said, 'Sorry, nurse, I find it hard to piss in the company of men, let alone women.' In such a dazed state, I shouldn't have cared less, but I knew it was not going to be easy to piss while she stood there. Not taking kindly to rejection, the nurse turned away in a huff and went off to do some other jobs.

I now concentrated on the task in hand, which I found extraordinarily difficult. I was still in an anaesthetised condition, and far too weak to even hold the container. My diddler was in a seriously minute state, not long enough to hang over the side of the bed, which meant that I couldn't just place the container on the floor and aim from there. I was also afraid that if I tried to reorganise myself into a better position, I was likely to slip and fall out of the bed. I was still wrestling with this quandary when the nurse pulled back the curtain and said, 'Have you finished yet?'

'Actually, I haven't started yet,' I replied.

'Well, anytime today would be good, Mr Riddle'.

I managed to get myself out of bed and onto the bedside chair. I had my willy dangling over the edge and the container underneath when in she came again. 'Mr Riddle!' she reprimanded, and once again left me alone. Her tone struck the boyish 'fear-of-disapproval chord' in my mind, and immediately my body responded, my tense muscles loosened, piss started splashing out and I felt such relief that I didn't ever want it to stop.

As the sheer joy of providing my urine sample was lasting longer than usual, I became quite anxious. The container was nearly full and I was still going strong. I tried my hardest to cut the flow, but my muscles were in no fit state to teach myself

83

new tricks. The container filled and filled, and as it spilled and spilled, all over my pyjamas and down onto the floor, the nurse walked back in.

Her silence was deafening. It took me a while but when I had gathered up the courage to look the nurse in the eye and try to excuse myself, she was already turning around to leave in an even bigger huff then before. She returned with a bucket and a mop and silently cleaned up the mess. She pulled back the curtains, put the white paper bag over the container, picked it up and walked away indignantly. Before she got to the ward door her stern silence broke into the most aggressive screech – the container had been so full that the contents had spilled out over the sides and all over her hands.

Nurses' nota bene: bring not one but two.

lamppost cleaner

I heard a story about this young lad who was approached by a policeman while up pissing against a lamppost. The policeman advised him to stop or be arrested. The young lad tried but alas could not. Taking this as an affront to his authority, the policeman grabbed the pisser by the collar and started dragging him away. The young lad grabbed onto the pole and pleaded that he was trying to wash grit off the pole. He was placed under arrest and when his case came up in court, the judge found him guilty of both a public order offence and for resisting arrest.

village idiot

A fellow lecturer and I were driving around Brittany in a camper van during our holidays from tutoring. We would drive to the next campsite along the coast every morning. Needing to pee I decided to do as I did whenever I needed to take a leak while driving; I opened the back door and exposed my genitalia to the beautiful passing countryside. I began pissing but the van slowed down and the countryside turned into a small village with its residents out on the

streets. I tried but couldn't stop. I thought of turning and pissing into the camper but all the bags were on the floor. Not knowing what to do I just continued pissing and braved the wrath of the villagers.

diet coke

A friend of mine who woke up earlier than his girlfriend one cold morning decided not to bother getting out of bed to empty his busting bladder in the toilet. Instead he pissed in the coke can next to his bed. When his girlfriend awoke late for work, she picked up what seemed to be an almost full coke can and decided to get her morning caffeine boost from that. Shocked and horrified at the saline taste, she twigged immediately what it was and avenged herself by pouring the remains over her boyfriend's face.

Due to the price of parking and the fear of losing a fare, New York taxi drivers never get out of their cabs to piss. They use catheters attached to their penises and piss into a bag which they empty at the end of the day.

Barbed Wire

One should not piss in the Amazon River because upon urinating, barbed shellfish, indigenous to the Amazon, can enter the urethra and lodge there. Infection and death will ensue if medical help is not sought. An operation consisting of cutting the shaft of the penis in half and removing the barbed fish must be performed if the patient is to survive.

drink piss take woman

The custom among the Tchuktchi tribe in Siberia is that a visiting male guest may sleep with any of the women providing he drinks a bowl of, or at least rinses his mouth with, her urine.

pissing in the ritz

I once had occasion to piss in the Ritz. I was taking a break from busking on my didgeridoo in the London underground and decided to view the town for a bit. I was walking up some street when the urge I had been restraining all morning came back at me with a vengeance. I started into a sprint and came upon some rather posh looking hotel. I got past the doorman and I saw the sign for the Water Closet. When I began making my way up the stairs, a tightly be-suited snooty looking woman snapped: 'Excuse me, sir, you cannot go up there.'

Pissing on the stairs would have got me in more trouble so I continued up the rest of the stairs saying, 'Come up and stop me.'

I rushed into the restroom and was totally taken aback: there was a balding man sitting by the door. I thought I might have to go back out and look for the ladies' but he didn't try to stop me. He just greeted me with a servile smile. I couldn't figure out what this well-dressed old man was doing in such a lavishly decorated latrine.

There were no urinals so I hurried into the cubicle and to my great relief, relieved myself. The porcelain was marble, the seat was African black wood, the wallpaper was a thick velvet curtain and the aluminium door handle was polished brass. 'You can always tell a tavern by its toilet' I thought. When I opened the ornately designed cubicle door this man was filling up the sink for me to wash my hands and neatly folding my own personal hand towel.

This was my first encounter with a toilet assistant and it made me wonder; how does one arrive at a job like this? Did he always aspire to be assigned as lavatory aid or did he fall on hard times? What kind of qualifications must one have to fill this position? No man, I thought, should end his days in this kind of employment. I took out some change and tipped this well-mannered servant of the Ritz, but it felt a bit odd putting thirty pence in coppers on a silver tray.

I left the hotel a bit bewildered and took up my position back in the tube station to collect pennies from passers by. As I began droning on the didge' I realised that my job and his weren't that different. We both provided a free service; me to passersby, he to passers of urine.

urine and sex

Viagra falls

A visiting tutor told me of a short-lived affair she had with a man who was into kinky sex. After about two weeks of meeting on and off he invited her for dinner in a posh restaurant and told her he'd booked a room in the hotel. All eager, she dolled herself up and wore her sexiest lingerie. Before dinner they both took some viagra pills and as they drank champagne they spoke of the dirty things they wanted to get up to. He told her he had one secret fantasy but would only tell what it was when they were upstairs.

Consumed by passion they could hardly contain themselves and they were at it as soon as they had closed the hotel bedroom door. After about twenty minutes she noticed that he was nowhere near ejaculating. She asked if everything was all right or if it was just the pills. He answered, 'Well, I told you I have a secret fantasy and it's the only thing that can make me come.' Ready for anything at that stage she invited him to reveal it. All excited he told her how he has fantasised about her pissing on him. Not too sure what to think she agreed after he offered to fulfil any of her fantasies in return.

They pulled back the covers and she straddled him and prepared to piss. But thoughts of the innocent chambermaid

91

having to clean up stopped her. He folded a few towels and put them on the carpet but again she couldn't. Not wanting to break the magic she said she'd drink a pint of water and wait until she was 'ready to go'. They rolled around on the carpet for a while until she said 'Ok! Let's try it in the shower.' Again nothing. She then told him it would probably be easier if she were sitting on the loo. So she drank another few glasses of water and he lay down, still aroused and over-excited, and put his head in front of the bowl and she sat right forward on the toilet seat.

By this stage her bladder was bursting. She was more eager to pee than he was to be peed on. After a few false alarms they both noticed that it wasn't going to happen. She thought their evening would just continue, but he got up, put his clothes on and stormed out of the room, leaving her sitting on the toilet naked and rejected. She was about to run after him but her bladder dam burst when the door slammed shut, and, as she put it, 'it was like Niagra Falls'.

piss douche

One of our college graduates got a lift from a trucker while hitching between Barcelona and Paris. As the journey wore on, the pair relaxed and began to talk. Their conversation touched on all the important issues of the day and when they were comfortable with each other's opinions they then got around to the subject of sex. Amongst the trucker's many tales of conquest was one about a young woman who derived immense pleasure from him pissing into her vagina. The trucker said he was reluctant at first, but after a few times he started getting into it himself. So every time after sex,

when his mickey was going into recovery mode, they would place towels underneath their bodies and he would enter her and urinate inside her. She assured the trucker that compared to the small amount of sperm ejaculated, she felt a far greater sense of climactic fulfilment.

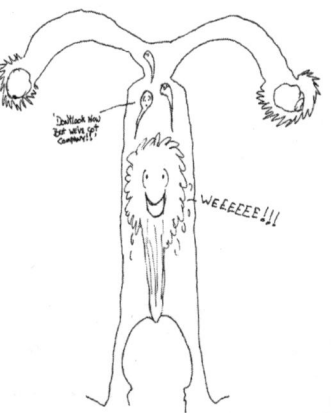

'DON'T LOOK NOW BUT WE'VE GOT COMPANY!'

WEEEEEE!!!

urinating contraception contraption

The previous story set my scientific mind to work. I went to the college library and read up on the pre-pill post-coital practice called douching. To avoid pregnancy women would flush the vaginal tract immediately after sex. Manufactured contraptions like bulb syringes and whirling sprays were once used to hose the tract with concoctions made from vinegar, alum, salt, soap and in some developing countries they still swear by Coca Cola. I began hypothesising. If douching actually worked and if urine could act as a spermicide, has this French woman's sexual quirk revealed nature's intended method of contraception, waiting all this time to be discovered?

The antidote is always next to the poison, dock leaves always grow next to the nettles, this may explain why we use the same gland to ejaculate and micturate.

Our piss: The most natural, least expensive and perhaps only erotic method of contraception?

Our penis: The best contraption for deploying this contraceptive liquid?

I rang a women's health centre and queried whether sperm could be destroyed by urine. Having never received such a question before, the helpful lady on the other end of the phone said she would have to call me back. This she did, and this is what I was told: when retrograde ejaculation occurs (when the spermatozoa is refluxed into the bladder), whether due to diabetes, surgery of the prostrate gland, or manually induced by squeezing the penis or by exerting pressure on the perineum at the point of ejaculation, the sperm will be destroyed by the urine in the bladder, and will later be emitted, impotent, during urination.

'That's wonderful,' I sighed. 'So I was right. One could use urine as a post-ejaculatory douche and be happy in the knowledge that no egg fertilisation will ensue?'

'No! You are quite wrong,' she replied, 'Although urine does destroy spermatozoa, douching has been proven to be an ineffective method of contraception and can actually aid the sperm's journey and propel them toward the cervix faster.' I thanked her for her time and put down the receiver all deflated.

There I was, the great Professor Jimmy Riddle, getting ready to dust off my hat and gown to present this great discovery at the next urine therapy conference in Singapore. But I suppose it was better to have found out now then be laughed at by rival schools. I'm not letting it go that easily, though. My next query will be: 'If a woman washed her vagina with her own or her partner's urine prior to sex could this have a spermicidal effect or could it hinder the eggs' ability to become fertilised?'

procreation V. urination

It is a widely held viewpoint that our purpose here on Earth is to procreate. Following from that we could therefore assume that the urge to spread our seed is, as one student put it, our 'primariest of primary urges'. But what happens when two fat primary urges want to have a go on the super slide at the swimming pool and there's room for only one in the chute? Well, they do as all boys do; they start having a scrap.

Ladies, I wonder if you have ever noticed how we men tend to love longer in the mornings? Yes, 'tis true, 'tis true. The fuller the bladder the longer-lasting the lover. So if you go at it before he gets up for a pee, the conflicting urges of ejaculation versus urination will confuse him, and a confused brain will ensure that nothing is released until one urge prevails over the other.

Nine times out of ten the urge to ejaculate wins. But when the urge to urinate is winning a man feels a pain in his shaft, which will make pelvic thrusts so sore that the erect penis will immediately begin to deflate so that urination may then commence. The man will be then left with the unbearable dilemma of faking an orgasm and running to the loo or being honest and running to the loo and we all know that being honest about a deflating erection will always be considered with a certain amount of suspicion.

sneezing and peeing

A sneeze is said to be as close to the feeling of death the average conscious man gets unless of course he gets involved in certain types of auto-erotic behaviour. The sensation of sneezing has been described as equivalent to one-sixteenth of an orgasm. But I have been warned, and so warn you, that sneezing when peeing does not notch the orgasmic sensation up by another couple of sixteenths. Instead you will feel a sharp pain in the abdomen.

This may be to your taste. Perhaps you're the type who prior to passing water attaches clothes pegs to their member, or squeezes it with a pliers, then claps and slaps it until it gets as red as a rhubarb. Perhaps you're one of those pervs who puts his mickey through bicycle wheel spokes, then upon commencing to piss starts spinning the wheel. Perhaps you didn't buy this book to read, instead you bought it to flagellate yourself. If you're looking for the most painful method of pissing here's one you won't recover from, one that will scare you for the rest of your days: next time you're on a farm take a piss on a live electric fence. You'll see then how turned on one can really be.

porn and piss

My theory is this: If we pissed through our ears no one, but the warped few, would find it erotic. But because we pee from the reproductive region there are many who find the association between the sexual organs and excretory orifices impossible to separate. Early experience of trying to catch a glimpse of a boy's or a girl's bits while they pee is

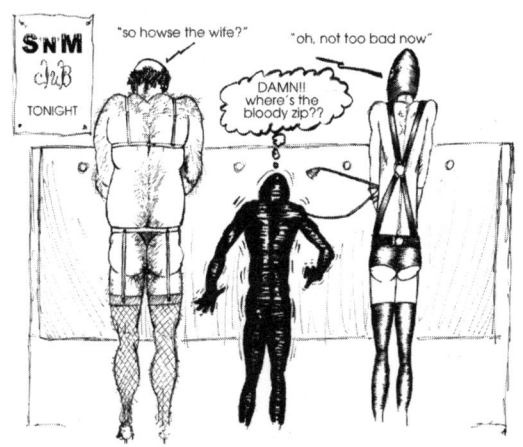

probably what starts most people off. Their earliest (and thus strongest) erotic memories are associated with the act of pissing. Anything to do with pissing; the sound, the odour, the sight of porcelain or even toilet paper will set the mechanisms of arousal in motion. In Tokyo, teenage girls' urine-stained undies can be bought from vending machines in metro stations, or from the enterprising schoolgirls themselves. Fetish clubs abound around the world. Even Dublin had its very own fetish club where along with a leather dress code and dark-rooms for gropers there was a pissing trapeze act; members of the audience would rush to get a space below and hold out their empty glasses to catch some of the golden spray. Meanwhile 'Missus Farty Pants' got on with his enema art/arse and they eventually got shut down.

The internet is full of porn sites dedicated solely to the act of urination. Male and female models are photographed pissing in their underpants or on the floor or in some cases into other models' open mouths. In extreme cases contraptions are built so that women can piss on their own faces and one such contraption enabled a woman to pee into her friend's mouth via her own anus. Do you understand this practice? If so, please don't ever explain it to me.

Sadomasochistic magazines go one further. In these you'll see submissive types succumbing to masterly figures, dressed in latex 'n' leathers, face masks and fittings, who whip them for being bold and shit on them for sport. But let me warn you budding sadomasochists, I have it on good authority that being slapped around the kidneys will have you pissing blood for weeks. And if you really want to aggravate your partner, eat loads of asparagus before you intend to piss on them – the smell is supposed to resemble cat's piss and will be as difficult to clean off.

acute cystitis

A cute disorder this is not. Acute cystitis, an inflammation of the urinary bladder, is caused by a bacterium from the enterobacteriaceae family (correct pronunciation earns you twelve exam points) called escherichia coli (six points), which normally resides inside our intestines.

The symptoms are fairly severe: a constant need to pee which, each time you indulge, turns out only to be a dribble which is accompanied by a nasty burning sensation (aaaahh!) – and that's if you're lucky, other times you'll be pissing blood. You also get a pain above the frontal pelvic bone, and cysts can form along the urinary tract, too. I won't go into chronic cystitis, but rest assured that it is very, very painful.

This is mostly a female phenomenon, but a small percentage of men also contract it. It is curable, through the use of antibiotics, but, as always, prevention is better than cure.

Ladies:

* Don't wipe from back to front (A to F – ass to fanny) after doing a crap. From fanny to ass is safer, and is preferable for your bottom because of the cleansing properties of fresh piss.

Men:

* You are responsible for inflicting a considerable percentage of the cystitis contracted by women. Dirty willies are dangerous. The smegma (cockage cheese) – which is made up of dead skin cells and genital secretions – builds up and inhabits the warm climate underneath the foreskin thus providing a rich breeding ground for bacterial growth.

I hereby issue a plea on behalf of the female race: men, boys and other males of the species, please wash willy wegularly!

And don't use the toilet paper you just wiped your bum with, or you too could contract cystitis. Soap and water clean very well and, if any priests are reading this, it doesn't count as masturbation, so no penance can be administered for this essential act of sanitation.

Men can also contract cystitis from anal intercourse. You won't if you wear a condom. But wearing the same condom could infect a woman if you are moving intercourse from orifice to orifice. If you're planning to do some hole hopping, all fanny to anus movements are safe, but when going the other way one should take off and replace a condom, clean or change a vibrator, use a different finger or … Ok, you get the picture.

Oh, and for all those deviants out there, e-coli is present in animal intestines too.

Some Words relating to piss from the dictionary of sex

* ***Accessory Urethral Canal:*** a second urethra that is found occasionally in the male penis. It is a birth defect and in most instances is nothing more than a blind pouch that extends a fraction of an inch along the shaft of the penis. Medical records show that some men have been born with two complete urethras extending to the bladder. An accessory urethral canal is often the site of a severe gonorrhoeal infection, requiring surgical removal of the extra urethra.

* ***Bulbitis:*** an inflammation of the urethra in the area of the bulb of the penis.

* ***Bulbospongious Muscle:*** a muscle that encircles the back of the penis and adjacent parts of the corpus spongiosum and corpus cavernosum. It acts to empty the urethra of urine after the bladder has been emptied, and its fibres also contribute to the erection of the penis by compressing the erectile tissue and deep dorsal vein of the penis during sexual excitement.

* **Colpocysitis:** an inflammation that involves both the vagina and the urinary bladder.

* **Dysuria:** a condition in which urination is painful or difficult, usually because of an organic disorder such as a spastic bladder.

* **Psychic Dysuria:** a term applied to an inability to urinate in the presence of other people.

* **Golden Shower:** a slang term for urination used in the context of sexual gratification obtained or sought from being urinated on or from drinking someone else's or one's own urine.

* **Mouse Unit:** a unit of measurement of gonadthropins in humans. It represents the amount of gonadthropin in a sample of human urine that, when injected into an immature mouse, will cause the weight of the uterus to double in four days.

* **Mutual Micturition:** a post-coital practice heterosexual couples engage in, which challenges them to urinate simultaneously into the same toilet.

* **Paradoxical Incontinence:** urination that occurs as a result of intra-abdominal pressure, a complication of

 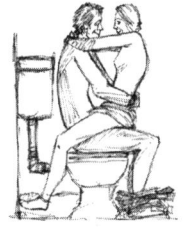 

prostatic hypertrophy (over-growth). In untreated prostatic hypertrophy, the bladder wall becomes thicker and capacity is reduced, resulting in a large amount of residual urine and difficulty in completely emptying the bladder in single urination.

* **Penile Clamp:** a clamp designed to fit over the penis as an aid in the control of urinary incontinence. The clamp is released periodically to allow urine to flow through the urethra.

* **Picket-Fence Injury:** medical jargon for a type of injury to the vagina that results from insertion of foreign objects during masturbation. Sharp or breakable objects can rupture the wall of the vagina, producing the kind of impalement that would occur if the woman fell astride a fence. Depending upon the angle of insertion of an object, it may puncture the urinary bladder or bowel as well as the vagina, which shares walls with those organs.

* **Privy Queen:** a homosexual male who frequents public toilets in search of trade.

* **Urethra:** the channel through which urine passes from the urinary bladder.

* **Urethral Chill:** a chill experienced by persons as a result of the entry of foreign products into the circulation via the corpus spongiosum. The urethral chill is often associated with the insertion of catheters or instruments into the penile urethra. It may also be a sign of damage to the lining of the urethra, permitting urine, pus or other substances to infiltrate the surrounding tissue.

* **Urethral Eroticism:** a psychoanalytical term for sexual pleasure accompanying urination. A person who remains fixed at the urethral stage of psychosexual development may develop fantasies or wishes concerning urinating on other people, or being urinated on.

* **Urethral Stage:** a stage in psychosexual development that occurs between the anal and phallic stages, when the urethra becomes the prime erogenous zone and sexual pleasure is gained by urinating. At this stage the child frequently comes into conflict with the parents over bladder training and feels humiliated when he or she cannot exercise control or wets the bed.

* ***Urinary Catheter:*** a catheter that is inserted through the urethra to drain the bladder to prevent the complications of urinary retention, as after surgery. Catheters are also used to inject radiopaque substances into the urinary tract for x-ray studies of organs and tissues in the genitourinary tract.

* ***Urination and Sex:*** a term referring to the observing of urination (in male or female) – an early and surreptitious expression in sex and the sex organs. In some instances this interest may develop into a paraphilia known as 'urolangia'.

* ***Urinism:*** a sexual practice in which urine, or urination, plays a part in the sexual act, as in urinating on one's partner, watching the partner urinate during foreplay or urinating during inter- course (women only), or smelling urine on the body or clothes of the partner.

* ***Urolangia:*** a sexual deviation, or paraphilia characterised by a

morbid attraction for the urine or urinary process of the sex partner or other individuals. Sexual stimulation may be experienced by watching the partner urinate. By sniffing garments smelling of urine or by yielding to one's desire or the partner's desire to be urinated upon.

* **Urophilia:** a psychosexual disorder consisting of an obsessive interest in urine and urination as a source of sexual excitement.

* **Verumontanitis:** an inflammation of the verumontanum, located on the floor of the urethra near the prostate. Among the causes are excessive sexual activity (including masturbation), prostatitis and seminal vesculitis. If swelling blocks the ejaculatory ducts, the man may experience pain radiate to the lower back, perineum and scrotum. Urinary frequency and premature ejaculation are sometimes caused by verumontanitis.

* **Water Sports:** a slang term referring to sexual fascination with urine and urination, often abbreviated as w/s.

jimmy riddle's
inventions

hover pants

I've designed a great invention that would ease the domestic tension caused by whether a simple plastic seat is raised or not. But perhaps, like most men, I'm too eager to solve problems where women are just as happy complaining. Yea well, here it goes anyway.

Hover pants are underwear with a detachable Velcro crotch on a pair of double-layered Lycra pants with a thousand minute perforations on the under side and a slim multi-speed rechargeable power pack. When turned on, jets of air strong enough to keep a woman gently hovering above any toilet seat will be emitted. Women in the future will therefore be able to enjoy the cosy feeling of pissing on a warm cushion of air.

somnambulator's piss encapsulator

Piddling somnambulators don't merely sleep walk – they piss walk. Yes, this is an all too frequent occurrence amongst the somnambulating community, and especially when they're drunk. Therefore, to save on laundry bills all over the world, I have invented the somnambulator's piss encapsulator.

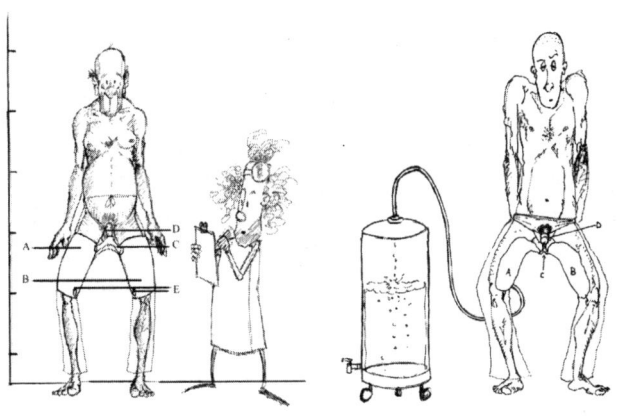

A self-adjusting penis nozzle (D) is secured to tight-fitting underwear (made from breathable fabric) to hold the wandering willy in place at night. Screwed into this nozzle is a one-way valved Y-Tube (C), which is attached to two air-tight, leak-proof and heat-proof plastic foil bags (A, B) which are secured inside double-lined silk pyjamas (long or short). A comfortable night's sleep with no slippage or spillage is guaranteed. In the morning all you need do is empty the bag, via the decanting taps on the outside of the silk pyjamas legs. Or you could attach the innovative 'riddle hose™' (E) and drain into any standard stainless steel water boiler or into the toilet itself. Another great leap forward in urine design from the College of Pissology.

the riddlette

Most women would only be too glad to have the option of pissing standing up. No longer would they feel vulnerable and undignified crouching in side-streets and alleyways, or risk getting nettle stings in ditches or fields. This is for women who by now should be fully green with penis envy.

The riddlette is an undergarment with an attached penile shaped tube of similar elasticity. It is custom designed by Professor Riddle to fit all fannies, with a simulated foreskin pressure gauge, made from self-cleansing industrial grade polyfibres. Its most popular feature is the simulated foreskin which, when pulled back, will speed up the jet.

Jimmy Riddle's Willy Wipes

No more shaking, no more dribbles down your legs, we in Riddle Incorporated have designed a breakthrough in men's sanitary products.

Willy wipes are sheets of extra absorbent paper towels. They will be encased in acrylic boxes (with individual locks), in every toilet throughout the land. They'll be attached at shoulder height to the wall, and a little to the left of each urinal. A matching dark acrylic box will be attached just above the urinal so you can dispose of your wipe discreetly.

From now on wiping one's willy at the urinal will not attract castigating looks from men pissing beside you. They will actually be counting their blessings, because sufferers of last dribbles have been known to lose control and beat those next to them senseless.

So, all together now chaps, let's hear you chant, 'willy wipes, willy wipes, we want willy wipes!'

the urinalette

Standing some two feet above most urinals men often fail to force the entire jet in the one direction without any spillage or spray. If only toilets could also act as urinals.

Enter the Riddle Inc. patented urinalette dual-usage urinal and toilet in one. There is no need for a seat; it's all in the lid.

Lift the lid and side wings appear. Men can now piss directly at the back of the lid safe in the knowledge that the wings will catch any spray.

The toilet will only flush after the lid has been let back down because the new flushing system occurs from underneath the lid and not from the porcelain.

The lid has retractable centre doors so when one needs to sit down the lid acts as the seat.

showerinal

Wondering whether one should or shouldn't piss in the shower will no longer be a matter of conscience nor will showerers need to worry whether they are standing in the previous person's piss because I, Jimmy Riddle, the toilet solution man, have designed a new system that can be fitted, at a nominal fee of course, in every household shower.

The showerinal is similar to those small wall indentations that hold soap. I will dig out and retile a large enough space, in the shower wall, in which one could sit or hover. I will attach and hide its own little pipe and route it to the main sewage pipe.

Taking a shower will now be more enjoyable then ever.

At the World Toilet Summit in Singapore during 2001, Japanese designers demonstrated a toilet that could make an automatic analysis of your urine and provide you with a printout before you left the restroom.

Pissing Problems

the last dribble

It has been the curse of man since the dawn of time. Since he first donned some fur or fig-leaf covering, he has been stuck with this malediction; the last dribble always goes down his leg. Can you imagine how annoying it must have been for stone-age man, just into britches, out on the hunt when, 'Hgnughrapf!' (Uh-oh!) – an urge in the groin area tells him he must stop.

'Fhargp? Uhgh!' (Huh? Oh) – something wants to get out. 'Rahgfp urgh hsapftark!' (I wish someone would invent zips!)

He produces his 'wabalikalongfrigadong' (meaty member) takes a leak: 'Mf mf mf mf mf mf mf,' (Aaaaaah) replaces it and goes back to the hunt. Suddenly a grunt turns into a roar, 'Fpu? Guf? Ufpragraystagnarsejeta! grahaagrgraah!' (Oh bother, dash and sloppy damn weather), and in an instant all the animals in the bush have run away. The other hunters run up to him. 'What's-gthe-gfucking-gstory? Gye-prick! Ghow-gthe-gfuck-dje-gthink-gwe're-ggonna-gkill-gany-gfucking-ganimals-gif-gyou-gkeep-gfucking-gblowin-gyer-gbleendin-gtop?' Amidst a storm of violent howls, yelps and somersaults they hear him say, 'Ugn-gfucking-glast-gngfucking-gdribble!'

Not much has changed since then, except that we now

react to this evil occurrence a lot more passively, yet an inborn primal instinct remains deep inside us, and sometimes we'd just love to beat the shit out of the person nearest to us. The twentieth century has not been too kind to us men either. It has brought us such amazingly useful inventions as the electric toothbrush, the electric tippexer, the gas-powered picture frame and, of course, the hot-air willy drier, which has the following legend inscribed on a metal plate stuck to its casing:

1. Shake excess water from willy.*

2. Press button.

3. Place willy under drier.

The things are bloody hopeless. They're always too high up, and by the time you manage to haul yourself up and balance yourself – hands on box, knees against the wall, thus exposing your willy to the warm wind – the friggin' useless contraption has stopped. Knowing that you'll fall if you take away your hand to press the button again, you hang there in midair, hoping it was a short-circuit and that maybe it will switch itself back on at any moment. Alas, you are, as usual, wrong. You

---

* A useless endeavour, as the more you shake the more you'll shake out, and the dribbles always hit you in the face.

must now let yourself carefully down off the wall, try to shake the piss away and put the little lad away knowing that you'll soon fall victim to that excruciating cold sensation of just one little drop of urine making its way gradually down the inside of your leg. 'Aaaaarghzuxnvtffgfxr!!!' (untranslatable).

There is hope. The twentieth century has actually invented something very useful, though largely under-utilised: toilet paper. This is, as women found out the minute that it first became available, the solution to both their own and men's greatest piddling problem. A sheet applied gently over the mouth of the penis will drain away and absorb the biggest and smallest of last dribbles.

But when you find yourself in a toilet with no paper to be

The first last dribble

found anywhere, there is a way to save the day; simply press the back of any fingernail against the tip of your penis. Due to the capillary action (solids tendency to attract liquid) that dreaded drop will roll over your nail and into the awaiting gaping urinal, and you will have done away with that scourge, the worst of curses, the last dribble.

You were going to wash your hands anyway, weren't you?

the dribbly willy syndrome

This has nothing to do with the above trauma and mainly affects those with foreskins. You have a dribbly willy; if it's all sploshy when you start peeing, i.e. it's like a spoon under a tap and the piss is going in every direction except toward the bowl.

To remedy this simply pull back your foreskin. This should correct your flow's trajectory immediately. But beware, this increases the strength of the jet – so aim down into the bowl before attempting this procedure.

If you can't pull back your foreskin without causing pain, you're either not using it enough or you've out-grown your sock – simply put, your foot's too big for your boot. This is a common masculine problem, for which there is a routine operation available. It'll only be sore for about a week and a half, and the benefits include a more hygienic willy (no more 'cottage cheese') and you will last longer when having sex. An orderly queue to the left please. But until that operation do remember one thing: If you sprinkle when you tinkle …

if you sprinkle when you tinkle

Women are always complaining that men don't lift the seat before they piss thus splashing all over it. If men do remember to lift the seat they are then given out to for forgetting to let it down again.

My good men, do not heed these grievances any longer. The professor has it on good authority that women don't even sit on those seats. I have often gone to the toilet after women and noticed that they were every bit as bad as their brothers. I'd a mind to ask them why they didn't practise what they preached but during the course of a conversation it was all revealed.

A college fresher told me of the ill fate that had befallen her in the toilets the night of our college ball. She was halfway through micturating when she realised that it was splashing off the lid and soiling her ball gown.

121

'How,' I asked her, 'did you not realise that you were sitting on the lid?'

'Well, they normally don't have them in toilets anymore and I never sit down, I just kind of hover.'

'What?'

'No one sits down on them.'

'Why not?'

'Well, at home I do, but never when I'm out. Actually not even at home anymore.'

'Why not?'

'Well, I don't want to sit on a previous hoverer's splashes.'

'But if all women in public toilets sat on the seats there'd be no splashes.'

'Yeah, but they don't... and even if they did, the flush leaves splashes too and we women can catch colds and infections far too easily when we expose our vulnerable genitals to germ-infested toilets.'

'But there are more germs on a toilet door handle than a toilet seat.'

'How do you know?'

'Well, I am a professor of pissology. But the essential question is this: If women don't sit on the seats why all the grief about men not lifting the seat?'

'Because the one time you do want to sit on the seat your little brother or one of his dopey friends has left a paddling pool of piss on the seat and it's just so aggravating to have to wipe someone else's smelly piss off the seat.'

'So what's all the noise about us having to let the seat down after we piss? Can't women do that themselves?'

'Well, we'd like men to be extra considerate because having only the one sphincter, in comparison to men's two, and a very short one-inch urethra in comparison to men's eight inches we have less time to do extra things before we pee. So if we choose to sit down, we do not want a good piss spoiled by landing on cold porcelain.'

'Ah, I see, so it's OK for women to leave splashes behind but men must be mannerly.'

'No, that's not true. I've never left a soiled seat for anyone. We women know all about being considerate. We've had to clean up after men's shit for thousands of years. Even when we lived in caves we women had to yada yada yada yada yada...'

Noticing I was about to enter one of those vicious scenes from the battle of the sexes, I discreetly changed the topic of conversation to revolutionary tendencies amongst captive dolphins in twelfth-century Prussia.

PS: The only resolution is this age-old argument is this:

If you sprinkle when you tinkle
Be sweet and wipe the seat.

how to piss without getting the string of the tampon wet

How do women piss without getting the string of the tampon wet? This issue was raised by my girlfriend who came out of the toilet, one day, extremely agitated. Being sensitive to the hardships of her monthly predicament (the word menstruate doesn't by any chance come from a marriage of the two words 'men' and 'castrate'?), I asked her what was bothering her. Her answer: 'Every time I go for a pee, the bloody string gets wet, and that wets my knickers and then I have this uncomfortable cold, wet patch on my skin.' So I sat her down beside me, gave her a cuddle and said I'd warm her up wherever she felt cold.

But my mind wouldn't rest – here was yet another puzzle for the pissing professor to solve – one that should be very easy to figure out.

The next time she needed to spend a penny I suggested she hold the string from behind but she returned with a similar expression of annoyance. I asked her had she not tried it? She replied, 'Yes, I did, but the friggin' thing came out, they're expensive you know…'

Next, I suggested she cut the string, but it still got wet. She kept cutting until it was as small as the wick on a candle, but she found it too hard to extract. So I stopped thinking and continued to warm her up instead.

A month or two later, while on a lecture tour of Germany, I asked some students if they had any methods for keeping the string dry. One student said that she would push the string back in around her anus, and that it would stay there for the duration of her pee. So I came back with this gem of knowledge to my girlfriend and – Da-da-daa! – it worked. Pity though, because I did enjoy warming her up.

Some pissing tips for Women

* If you see a man wearing a kilt in the ladies' loo, he's probably a Scotsman who thought the sign on the door read 'laddies'.

* If you see a sign saying 'Ladies to let', it's probably a brothel.

* Visitors to Ireland take heed, the toilet signs can be quite confusing; You may think that the 'F' in the loo marked *Fir* indicates a convenience for females or the fairer sex but you'd be wrong, *Fir* means Men. *Mná*, has the same letters as man, but actually means Women.

* Wear a ring on your middle finger to remind yourself you're wearing a g-string – a very common complaint is that women forget they have them on, and the piss just splashes everywhere.

* When out at some social gathering, and the queue is too long for the ladies', just go to the men's. The men's have twice as many repositories, meaning there's generally a cubicle free. Men seldom mind and porcelain refuses no bottom.

* Forget silent pissing, why not have some fun and make some noise instead? A girl I know told me she could accelerate her pee right up to jet speed, and slow right down to dribbles, just by squeezing and releasing her pelvic floor muscles. You can just imagine bashful Japanese women discarding their normal behaviour and pissing along to the pop songs playing on the toilet radios: splosh splosh, stop, splosh dribble, splosh ... Or female Hare Kr'snas could piddle their chant: Splosh splosh, dribble dribble, dribble splosh, dribble splosh, dribble dribble, splosh splosh, splosh dribble, splosh dribble ...

* An elegant older lady asked me to warn young women not to socialise wearing full-body undergarments with buttons at the crotch because they are an absolute toilet-time scourge. Not taking her advice at face value I suggested she could replace the buttons with some sort of self-adhering material. But she rejected that idea with this eloquent assertion: 'Retracting my pubic hair from a sticky surface is going quite beyond my desire to suffer for sophistication and who wants to be socialising while their short and curlies are being terrorised by Velcro?'

how to pee half-asleep

The humble potty is probably the second greatest toilet training tool ever invented (this book, of course, being the greatest).

For years it has acted as an excellent preliminary step for little bums, preparing them to perform on the big stage; the great anal amphitheatre. Prior to its invention, only affluent parents could protect against their little 'uns falling down into the toilet and drowning in the sewers, by decking them out with miniature life jackets.

The potty, however, needn't be discarded as an apprenticeship appliance assisting the un-advanced. It can still be utilised on occasion as a urinal to enable you to piss in your sleep without wetting the sheets.

You know the feeling you get; you're in bed, all warm and cosy, when suddenly you feel the urge to pee? You are struck with that terrible dilemma of not wanting to leave the warmth of the bed yet knowing that you won't sleep much more with such a bulging bladder. A rude disturbance of a good night's sleep is always the outcome.

To achieve a balance between the warmth of the bed and the cold of the toilet, the inactivity of slumber and the waking activity of pissing, do like a mother of a student of mine does – put a potty (the much larger size) underneath your bed, and when the urge arises drag a blanket off the bed, wrap it around you, slip out the potty, sit down, still warm and dreamy, and do away with the scourge until morning.

I myself often use a piss bottle and if I'm halfway through a snooze and dreaming of walking towards a toilet, I've trained myself to instinctively reach for the bottle, unscrew the top, throw my legs out over the side of the bed, sit up and piddle away dreamily. When I'm finished I screw the top back on and resume my snooze, unhindered.

It is essential that you empty and clean your container every morning after use. If you don't, the smell will be so foul and so revolting the next time you use it that it will wake you from the sleepy state you were so desperately trying to keep.

how to piss with the use of only one hand

THE EXPERT   THE NOVICE   THE DISASTER

If one hand is either dirty, wet, infected, bleeding, fingerless, busy holding a telephone, paper or cigarette, or encased in a frame since it shook hands with Mohammed Ali, the pope or me, Jimmy Riddle, there is a way of doing the entire deed with only one hand.

To unzip: just pull the zip down. If that causes trouble: place your thumb between the folds, under the button, push thumb up, then push zip down with your middle finger. If you're not wearing any underwear beware when re-zipping; it can cause nipping (which is excruciating). If you're wearing centre-slit boxer shorts you'll be much safer and should have no trouble pissing. But if you're wearing your girlfriend's panties, or just your regular jocks or Y-fronts, do not take your John Thomas out from the side, nor through the central passage in the Y-fronts that erecting willies always make their way through. Many problems arise when taking it out. For instance, it can get stuck halfway out, causing you to urinate down the side of your leg; it could get squashed between your thigh and the side stitching possibly stopping the flow, and all the urine that has built up will go all over the place upon its release.

The correct way to take out your diddler with one hand is from the top. Push the underwear elastic out and down with your middle, marriage and little fingers. Do not rest the elastic under the sac because you may suffer the flow obstruction problems outlined above. Now, with your thumb and index finger, take hold of your willy, aim it and piddle away to your heart's content. Re-zip cautiously, and don't forget to wash your hand!

how to piss if both hands are fully plastered

'DON'T LOOK AT ME...
I HAVEN'T TOUCHED IT IN WEEKS!'

**A MAN ASKS POLITELY
FOR HELP WITH HIS DILEMMA**

If you find yourself at a urinal with both hands in plaster casts you'll either have to go in your pants or ask some helpful member of public to assist you. However, if that person were me I would be very wary. I'd be wondering how you got your trousers on, buttoned and zipped in the first place.

To avoid this dilemma, you should wear tracksuit bottoms and if you had been thinking ahead, you'd have asked for something like a coat hanger hook to be attached to the palm side of the plaster so you could rest your diddler on that. But I've no idea how you could pose the question properly:

'Excuse me? I just can't seem to... I'm not a... you know... but I really... could you... ?'

how to piss with no hands at all

There are some amazing people in this world of ours – people who can write, dress, undress, play snooker, make cups of tea (two sugars and a drop of milk please), drink, eat, and all with their feet. Certainly they can lift skirts, undo zips, pee sitting or standing and wipe as well. Compared to some of these people, those of us with a full

complement of hands are the disabled ones, so I don't need to tell them how to do it, they know much better than I.

the two-tiered pee

Now this is a difficult one. You see, as grows the young man so grows his weaponry, and when his gland is swollen after choking the chicken or porking, his little fishy's lips protrude that little bit more altering the natural physiology so that the one-eyed jap now has two.

So when fine fluid must flow it arrives not in mono but in stereo, but being too loud for the arena, spillage from one if not both streams is imminent and no matter what cock choreography or dicksy dancing is executed straight roads may lead to Rome but these kamikazes fly right by. To remedy this, the giant must be brought to his knees and his skinhead friend must be forced to plunge into the aquarium. Then and then only will correct piddling non-spilling procedures be adhered to.

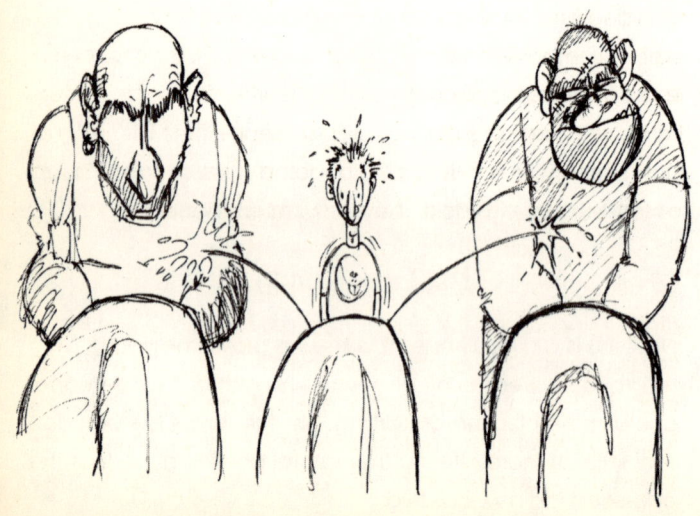

proximity pissing

Some men, as we all know, stand at a urinal, whip out their langer, shake it a bit, and immediately begin pissing. But this doesn't work for me. I've tried running cold water over my hands, followed by the two-shake shimmy (three shakes is a wank). I've coughed and even tried spitting to encourage the fluid to flow, but all to no avail. I don't understand why, but pissing in close proximity to someone else is one skill I have been unable to master. Looking at it objectively, all I've got to do is pee. I mean, what could be simpler than that? But to this day, despite my exhibitionism in other areas, if I need to take a leak and there's a cubical free, that is where I pee. Too often I'd be standing at a piss pot, with someone next to me, and I just wouldn't be able to get it together at all. I'd usually just pass it off with the Bono in the loo impersonation – 'Ah well, stage fright again' – and leave with a full bladder.

The worst of these experiences happened while I was on crutches upstairs in McDaid's pub. Now, if there are fifty in the bar it's full, but on this occasion there were at least 150 crammed into it. I had a pint and a half on me and needed to bleed the lizard, but getting through the crowd on crutches seemed a complete impossibility. By the time I'd finished my second pint, I was really bursting, so I got up, checked my balance (not good) and hopped through the cluster of humanity, causing much grief by holding on to people's shoulders and nearly spilling their pints.

I hopped up the steps to the toilet and opened the door. Happily there was no one there, so I went to the nearest of the two urinals. My good leg was very, very tired and my bladder about to burst. I'd just whipped out my diddler when in walked some bloke. 'Oh fuck!', I said to myself. I closed my eyes and thought of all the water in the world, every lake, pond, tap, pool and waterfall, but for the life of me I just couldn't pee, I just couldn't. The only alternatives were to either wait there, dick in hand, doing nothing until he'd gone; or turn around and go into the cubicle, which would be against men's room etiquette, and would make me feel like an even bigger wally.

So I just repeated my Bono impression, stuffed the beggar back in out of the cold, hopped back down the steps, and into the bar, squeezed through more people, spilling much of their drink, and managed to get back to my seat. Leg and bladder aching, I sat there in pain for the rest of the night. It wasn't until we left the pub much later on that I relieved myself against a wall, and my oh my, what a relief it was.

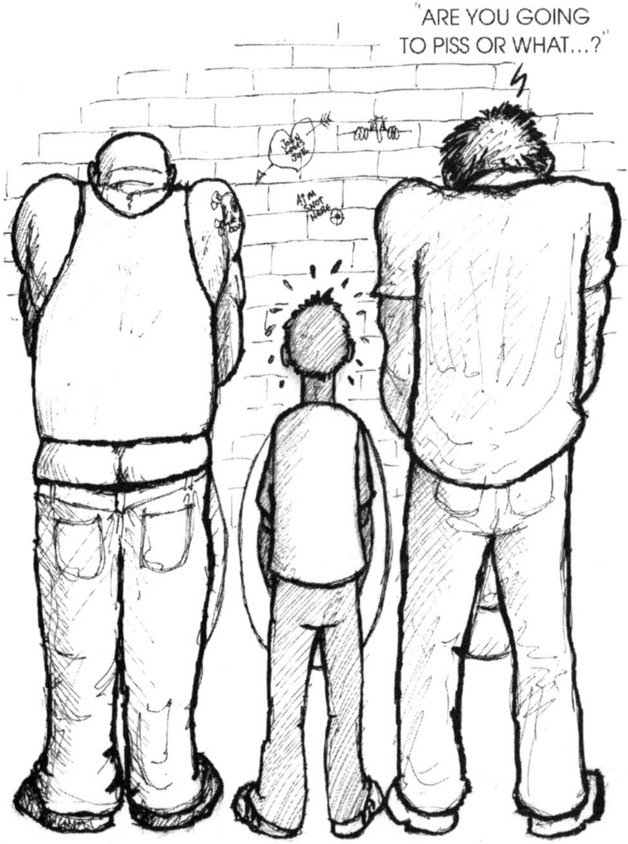

Bashful Bladder Syndrome: the cause and the cure

I read up on the work of two esteemed practitioners, Allan N. Schwartz CSW, PhD and Ronald Pies MD. Both are experts who specialise in helping people pee in crowded restrooms. Apparently I'm not alone in this. There are reportedly 19 million sufferers of what is medically known as 'Psychogenic Urinary Retention', 'Paruresis' or 'Bashful Bladder Syndrome' (BBS).

Bad experiences in youth such as being ridiculed at school or pressurised by parents, can set off this form of anxiety. BBS can be very debilitating as I, and many others, have discovered. Discomfort at the proximity of other pissers, the embarrassment of spending too long doing nothing coupled with the fear of being heard destroys our God-given right to an unencumbered piss.

Others get BBS because they fear that their tackle is being scrutinised. These poor souls also imagine that those close by can read their thoughts! In the worse cases it can actually destroy people's social lives causing them to stay at home for fear of encountering that dreaded moment.

Pissing should be an involuntary act that is blocked only if there is some serious physical impediment. But no matter how much you need to piss, if you've got BBS, your body will resist.

BBS sufferers can be cured in a number of ways:

* They can be desensitised by gradual exposure to situations which resemble the one they fear.

* Biofeedback can help too but you'll have to read the 1991 issue of 'Urology' online to find out what that is.

* There are three self-help books *Free to Pee, Shy Bladder Syndrome*, and my favourite *Feel the Fear and Do it Anyway.*

* Nicholson Baker, in his book *The Mezzanine*, mentions a method to deal with this situation: in short, one must imagine the head of the guy pissing next to you in the urinal and then piss on it. With this petty act of malicious imagination, you should begin to piss.

* The pharmaceutical industry has come up with some expensive pills that may or may not work. Bethanechol supposedly makes the bladder contract, while Atenolol is a blood-pressure medicine that can counter anxiety.

I am happy that the pharmaceuticals are taking this issue seriously, but there is no way in hell any doctor is going to prescribe the professor with pills in order to piss. So, next time I'm at the urinal and there's someone beside me, I'm going to take as long as I want. I don't care anymore, even if it takes half an hour. I'm going chant out loud:

This is my wonderful workaday willy
The dew will be drained from the lily
Whenever it feels quite ready.

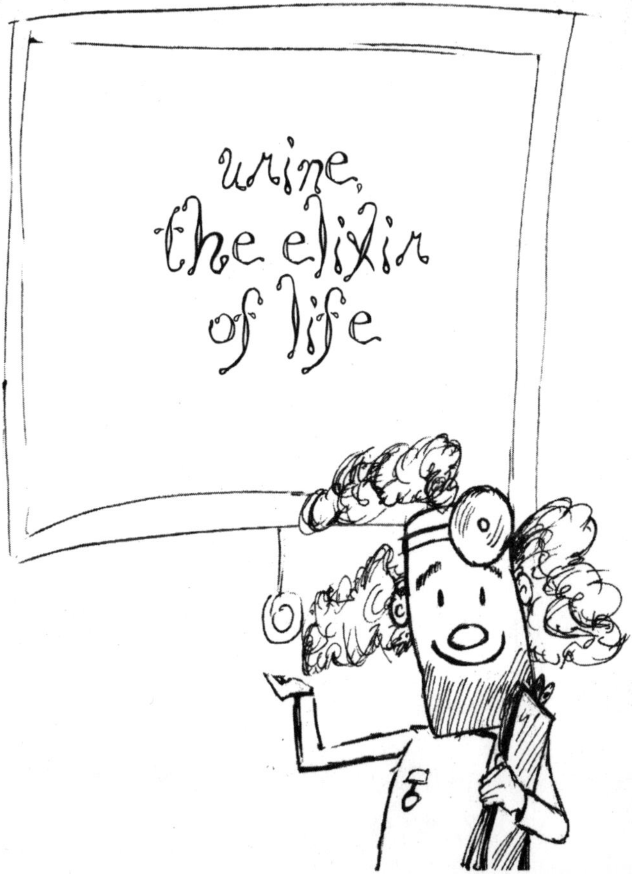
urine,
the elixir
of life

rashes and actresses

In the winters before my father was given his first pair of long trousers, he used to suffer from inner thigh rashes that were due to the frosty weather and the harsh material of the shorts rubbing against his tender young skin. The remedy prescribed in his hometown of Carlow in the 1940s and 1950s was urine. Pissing on his rashes, he told me, would make them go away.

He also told me that a famous actress, who was in the film *The Playboy of the Western World*, admitted being cured of many allergies and ailments after drinking a glass of her own piss everyday. Mmm, I can just taste it now – that strong, salty, acidic bile flavour rolling down my throat; the warm, pungent vapours rising from the blood-yellowed liquid and the sewage waft filling my nostrils …

I mean, for God's sake, who in their right mind would drink their own piss? OK, I know that if you were stuck in a desert you'd be forced to drink your piss, and yes, I know you could survive on it, but who in their right mind…? The body is getting rid of it, it obviously doesn't want it any more.

However, what my father told me prompted me to do some research with the result that my initial distaste has somewhat altered.

the history of piss drinking

People have been drinking their own piss since the beginning of time – well it was actually twenty past the beginning of time when Adam felt his first urge to urinate. Intrigued as to what was happening, he pointed his mickey upward so he could get a better view. Mouth agape with anticipation he unwittingly began pissing, but before he could avert the direction of the stream some of this precious liquid landed down his throat and he immediately felt better. Eve was very discouraging of this practice and so Adam continued to give himself the health benefits in secret. Eve ate the apple whereas Adam drank his piss. He passed the knowledge on to Cain and Abel who in turn passed it on to us. But since Eve's initial discouragement of this practice it has always remained a secretive activity.

Thanks to the internet there are no secrets any more. Click onto urine therapy and you will learn why to drink it, what part of it to drink and when and when not to drink it.

You will read the sceptics' and the adherents' angles on the whole subject. You will read about Martha Christy's miraculous recovery from being one of the sickest women in history to becoming an author and natural healthcare consultant. You will learn that urea is used in most moisturisers, that uric acid may actually cure cancer, that urine is a clean sterile liquid full of medicinal properties and the better the quality of food you eat the better the medicinal properties of your pee.

There are even quotes from the Bible:

Drink water from thine own cistern.
(John 7:37).
If any man thirst, let him come unto me, and drink ... out of his belly shall flow rivers of Living Water.
(John 4:14).

These quotes would suggest to me that Jesus, himself, promoted such a practice.

* There is information from ancient Chinese medical texts on how to crystallise urine to make it easier to swallow.

* You can learn how Aztec physicians used urine to clean and disinfect external wounds and administered it as a drink to relieve tummy and intestinal problems.

* Find out how Tibetan doctors can diagnose an illness with their historic 'urinalysis'.

* There's the Yogic practice called *Shivambu* to which a late Indian prime minister attributed his health and longevity.

* There's the Japanese therapeutic practice of performing an enema using one's own urine.

* Last, but far from least, there's the Tantric piss-drinking practice called *Amaroli*. This comes with steps to take before attempting it, and, they boast, if you continue the practice for ten years you will be able to fly through the air without effort!

Although I, Jimmy Riddle, am a professor of pissology my expertise, alas, is not in this branch of science. I can only conclude following my lengthy research that people are being

145

cured and are benefiting from the morning mid-flow.

I believe that it is not for others to criticise what they haven't tried. Yet I am also convinced that one should convince oneself before trying to convince anyone else of the benefits of drinking their own piss.

Some facts and warnings

No pain, no gain. Fresh urine is actually sterile, meaning it is devoid of any pathogens at all (except in the case of a urinary or kidney infection), and, for most people, there are no intoxicating side effects when consumed. But not everybody can jump right in and start drinking their own piss. The Chinese Association of Urine Therapy warns that beginners may suffer from diarrhoea, itching, pain, fatigue, soreness of the shoulder, fever, etc. These symptoms appear more frequently in patients suffering long-term or more serious illnesses, and symptoms may persist, generally lasting anything from three to seven days. Sometimes symptoms continue for up to a month, or even over six months. They put this down to recovery reaction and say that if one persists these difficulties can be overcome and the benefits of such a practice will eventually be enjoyed.

It is advised not to store urine overnight or in a fridge because stale urine provides fresh ground for bacterial growth.

A low-fat all-protein diet is not recommended because the nitrates in urine become highly concentrated making your urine very acidic, thus damaging your kidneys.

Avoid asparagus as it tends to break down into sulphur-containing compounds and imparts a putrid odour upon excretion.

Urine is formed in the nephrons of the kidneys, and is a liquid or semi-solid solution of metabolic waste containing 90% water with the rest made up of dissolved and suspended solids, none of which are toxic: urea, inorganic salts, creatine, ammonia, uric acid and pigmented products of blood breakdown, one of which – urochrome – gives urine its typically yellowish colour. Other elements include hormones, proteins, antibodies, melatonin and some other bene-ficial pharmacological agents.

the daily dosage

What is your daily dosage of piss? The dosage used by the estimated three million urine drinkers in China and two million in Japan is half a cup a day. They utilise the mid-flow of their morning's first piss. This is obtained by disposing of the first half-cup of urine and then refilling the cup. The liquid should then be sipped like tea and not swallowed like water.

internal applications

In my lengthy research I have come across and heard some fascinating employments and incredible cures claimed in the name of urine therapy. Here are some of the best.

* In his book *Scatological Rites of all Nations*, published in 1891, J. C. Bourke wrote that in the seventeenth century,

  One's own urine was drunk as a preservative from the plague ... and as a drink for lues Veneries (syphilis).

* In the same century, Michael Etmiller wrote:

  The urine of a boy twelve years old who had been drinking wine was placed in a receptacle, surrounded by horse dung for forty days, allowed to putrefy, then decanted upon human ordure, and distilled in

an alembic. The resulting fluid was looked on as a great 'anodyne' (pain reliever) and used for scurvy, hypochondria, cachexy, yellow and black jaundice, calculi of the kidney and bladder, epilepsy and mania. It was taken both internally and externally.

* Also in eighteenth-century Europe, human (and cow's) urine, was used to cure rheumatism, gout, dropsy, sciatica, asthma, periodontitis, and to prevent influenza and pestilence.

* John Armstrong's book *The Water of Life* (1971) mentions that Europeans have recently been adding human, cow or pig urine to the more upmarket facial soaps.

* Historically urine was used to break down blood clots. It was also used as a sleep aid, to cure yeast infections, fever, oral infections and diabetes.

* In the present day there is a specialist in Los Angeles who charges insecure movie stars large fees for injecting them with their own urine. One such actress decided to economise and drink her own urine instead. She also used it as a facial lotion. Her son, however, could not be persuaded to use urine therapy and said he'd rather suffer his asthma than undergo this treatment.

* Doctor G. K. Thakkar, an Indian urine therapist, says that 'this free, yet priceless therapy will prove to be a boon to our poor country; it is a therapy which is capable of curing a host of diseases ranging from common cold to cancer and from arthritis to AIDS.'

* Amoebic dysentry, apart from giving you a severe dose of the shits, can also cause the intestines to perforate and abscesses to appear in the brain, testes, liver and bones. Prior to medical treatment, a fifty percent mortality rate was the norm. But I am informed that a friend of a friend, who contracted AD whilst travelling in Africa many miles from the nearest hospital, was told by a local villager to drink his own piss. This he did and he was cured of this serious illness.

* NASA's answer to the lack of fresh water on its eighteen-month manned mission to Mars is to get astronauts to drink their own urine. Albeit recycled, filtered and purified.

* The water Londoners drink is said to be the city's inhabitants' own urine recycled seven times. (Is that why they all have *cock*ney accents?)

* Fertility drugs contain estrogens from human urine that stimulate ovulation in women and sperm production in men.

* Serono Laboratories in Italy use the urine of post-menopausal nuns to prepare the pharmaceutical extract Pergonal, prescribed for fertility.

* Many women receiving hormone replacement therapy are receiving doses derived from horse urine. One such is Premarin, which is a preparation made from mares' urine.

* Gargling one's own urine is supposed to cure most throat inflammations.

* Baboons' urine is consumed in beer by a Zimbabwean tribe in the belief that it acts as an aphrodisiac.

external applications

* Rubbing urine into one's balding scalp is supposed to re-fertilise the follicles and get hair growing again.

* Natural blondes can brighten dulling locks by washing them with urine. This is what one mother advised her daughter to do in the 1950s in county Clare.

* Piss is a natural antiseptic and was used as a steriliser in hospitals in the seventeenth and eighteenth centuries.

* Islanders off the coast of Ireland pissed on their hands to cure the cuts they sustained when pulling in fishing nets.

* Peeing after a kick in the testes alleviates the pain.

* Washing your willy with your own urine will greatly reduce the risks of contracting venereal diseases.

* If you suddenly happen to sit on a sea urchin, and the island doctor is away on holiday and the helicopter rescue team is busy saving a drowning fish, pissing on the affected area will kill the poison in the needles. How you are supposed to piss on your own bum is another problem. Crouching down and pissing on some rocks, hoping that some splashes will hit your butt, is one way. Robbing a young child's castle-building bucket, pissing in it and pouring that onto the affected area is another. But if the shock of such an experience shuts down the pissing duct, you could always ask a trusted friend to piss on your bum for you.

* Rubbing piss on a jelly-fish sting is said to cure you of the pain and poison.

* A purported cure for chilblains is to piss on the area affected.

UREA: a nitrogenous compound found in the urine of mammals and produced through protein decomposition. $CO(NH^2)^2$

* One cure for athletes' foot is to wash the toes in urine.

* Rubbing fresh piss on sunburn will ease the pain and soothe the skin.

* Eczema, psoriasis and other rashes can be eased by rubbing urine on the effected area.

* Pee is said to be good for replenishing lank and lacklustre hair.

* A purported cure for chapped lips is to rub urine on them – sure you won't be doing any kissing anyway.

* An alternative cure for a verruca is to wash it with urine.

* Welders, I am told, piss on their hands before beginning a job, for reasons I have yet to find out.

* Some trapeze artists piss on their hands to retain callouses, to toughen up hands and stop infections from cuts.

* Victorians would wash their hands with urine to soften them.

* Guitarists – there's no need to build up callouses on your fingertips in order to play perfect sounding chords. Pissing on your fingertips or dipping them in the piss you're about to drink, is said to do the job just as well.

* Washing one's face with urine is said to clear away acne.

* Indigenous Americans encountered in 1806 by Lewis and Clark's expedition to Oregon had the custom 'of bathing themselves all over with urine every morning.'

* Many modern Japanese women are said to engage in urine bathing.

* Many of the claims made above are to do with the application of urine onto the skin and here is the most likely reason why it works: the presence of urea in the urine is the result of the body's chemical balancing of sodium chloride and water ratio. Urea is one of the best and only medically proven, effective skin moisturisers in the world.

* Urea increases the water-binding capacity of the skin by opening skin layers for hydrogen bonding, which then attracts moisture to dry skin cells.

* Urea is commonly recognised as an effective antibacterial, antifungal and antiviral agent.

* When used on a wound, urea causes an osmotic imbalance that kills bacteria and fungus.

* Jack Dempsey, heavy-weight champion of the world, used to rub urine on his face to prevent cuts.

JACK DEMPSEY, WORLD HEAVYWEIGHT CHAMPION

pisstetious animal Behaviour

* Male Billie goats urinate on their own heads to make themselves attractive to Betty goats.

* A female rat will piss on her litter's heads, so that their father will recognise their mother's smell and not eat the babies. They also defecate around a certain area to mark boundaries for the little ones.

* To mark their territory, and so as not to get lost, dogs, as we all know, pee on as many poles and parked cars as they can.

* The concentration of ammonia in cats' piss, or even the steam of cats' piss could blind you if it came in contact with your eyes.

* Weil's disease (leptospirosis) is caused by the absorbtion of rat's piss. In its most severe form it can cause enlargement of the liver, inflammation of the kidneys, bleeding from the orifices and eventual death.

* Female dogs' urine discolours lawns. To stop them from doing this many gardeners leave bottles of water around the edge of the lawn.

stranger applications of piss

* In some parts of Africa urine is sprinkled on milk to keep it fresh, yet in India they do this to curdle milk for making cheese.

* During the First World War, soldiers without gas masks urinated on a piece of cloth and wore the cloth over their noses and mouths during a gas attack.

* Troops in the Second World War prevented trench foot by pissing in their boots.

* Urine was used for tanning leather.

* Before a thickening of wool was to commence, the inhabitants of villages all over Ireland would collect urine at *céilís* in buckets and then store it in big vats. All in attendance were encouraged to donate except those who had been eating onions. This practice of gathering piss possibly gave rise to the origin of the saying 'he wouldn't even give you the steam off his piss', which describes how mean some people are perceived to be.

* Urine of persons who had been eating cabbage was considered especially efficacious in scouring cloth.

* Stale urine was used as a detergent during the boom times of the linen trade in Ireland.

* Male salmon will be attracted to bait which has been dipped in a woman's pheromone-rich urine. This method of sex selection greatly helps retain river stocks during spawning season. Getting ovulating women to piss in the river may also be effective.

* Compost is greatly enriched by pissing in it.

* The concentrate liquid from the mixture of half a barrel of harvested comfrey or nettles and two gallons of urine will act as an excellent nitrogen-rich liquid fertiliser.

* Urine was used to cover the three components that make up gunpowder (sulphur, salt peter and charcoal) to stop them from separating in transit.

* The dye in the fifteenth-century Belgian tapestry of *The Unicorn and the Lady* was colour fastened to the wool with urine.

* Some American Indian artists piss on their bronze sculptures to enact the ureic chemical reaction that turns bronze green.

* Utilising the urine of cows that have been grazing on mango leaves creates the famous paint pigment Indian yellow.

fungi-flavoured urine

Fly agarics are said to be the most hallucinogenic of fungi but also the most deadly. Ingesting them straight out of the ground could poison and kill you. In order to achieve the hallucinogenic effects without being poisoned, novices must drink the urine of one who has built up a tolerance to the muscarine (the toxic substance). The potency of the muscimol (hallucinogen) remains unaltered having been secreted from the kidneys and does not decrease significantly until it has passed through the seventh drinker.

To communicate with the spirits, the indigenous people in Siberia drank the urine of another who had consumed the hallucinogenic mushroom, fly agaric.

Before going to war, it was the custom of the Turks to sacrifice the eldest and most feeble member of their tribe by feeding him fly agaric. Prior to dying from the poison the old man would piss into a container. Soldiers would then drink from this container and without any fear would march off to battle.

urine hunters

Stags and reindeers are often stalked in Scandinavian countries, not so much for their meat and fur but more for their urine. 'When it snows, little else but fungi grows', so the reindeers live on a diet of mushrooms. Fly agarics are in plentiful supply and have no ill effect on the animals which means that the poison gets absorbed and hallucinogenic properties pass out when they urinate. Scandinavian folk shadow these beasts until they pass water and then they rush over to the steam and gorge on the yellow snow. What happens next is anyone's guess, but Goblins, Orks and all sorts of monsters are said to appear!

möre piss tales

the autumn shroom hunt

Marlay Park is one of the many parks around the outskirts of Dublin that boasts large tracts of grass and beautiful vegetation. But every autumn, park-keepers notice that the usual smattering of prams and nannies are outnumbered five to one by straggling teenagers from all the housing estates in the south of the city.

This autumnal mushroom hunt is the reason groups of hunched, uniform-clad school kids looking over-interested in the grass are ordered to leave the park lest they want their names taken and added to a garda file as possible drug traffickers. The claim that they are NSPCA campaigners, ensuring that the soil is the right acidic level for worms, never seems to work and tends to get them thrown out even quicker.

So, the same group of teenagers thrown out in the day don big pocketed trench coats, equip themselves with torches and plastic *SuperCrazyPrices* bags and make their way to the park at night when the park-keepers are abiding union work hours and are sitting at home being mesmerised by the TV.

One such evening, a bunch of my students found a fresh crop springing up before their eyes. Having bagged enormous amounts and gorging just as much, the fun began. Eamon began trying to count to ten without repeating the number five, while Mark was busy calculating possible profits from freeze-drying them and selling them on the internet. Kate was pondering out loud why only schoolgirls wear pigtails, when Leo ran over to them screaming, 'My mickey! My mickey! I can't find my mickey! I went for a piss and me mickey is gone!'

After much laughter, he asked one of the lads to come over with a torch to check, but as none of the blokes would, Kate was handed a torch to help him find it. But before she could begin the search, Eamon heard it pissing in the bushes and they all rushed over to retrieve it, but it had escaped. Then Mark thought he heard it pissing in the stream so they all rolled up their jeans, took off their shoes and socks and ran in to search for his mickey there. But the sheer beauty of the colours and patterns distracted all but Mark from this very important mission. Mark, due to the cold water, was becoming even more eager to empty his tightening bladder.

He got out of the stream and ran over to the park-keeper's hut for fear that his penis was hiding in there and would be used against him as evidence. Much to his relief he found it there, but before he could shout out he saw Kate searching

163

in the shrubs beside him. 'I thought you were in the stream,' he said.

'Am I not?' she replied.

Not being too sure himself, he quickly changed the subject and told her that he'd found his mickey and was now able to pee. Without a sexual thought passing through his mind, he asked her if she'd shine the torch while he took a pee - for fear it might escape his grip again. But notions of a sexual nature were rushing through her mind and she insisted that she should hold it, because, she warned him, if he lost it once he would most definitely lose it again.

urination and humiliation

Is it not amazing how humiliating the simple act of urinating can be? The natural passage of bodily waste fluids directed with a malicious intent is considered amongst one of the most highly offensive acts of aggression. This is noticeable when victors of yore, to display their power, would piss on a beaten enemy, or to display contempt people would piss on a dead foe's grave. The sporting figure of speech 'we pissed all over them', meaning to win easily, might be a throw back to times when this practice actually happened on the battle field.

pee in her pants

What would it take for a woman to realise she should save herself and get out of a violent relationship? It can take years in therapy to re-build one's self-esteem to gain the courage to leave an abusive relationship. But for one young woman, whose story was related to me, it only took one final act of disrespect and overnight she made the decision to go.

In a bid to spice up their sex life, and perhaps their relationship, she bought some sexy new lingerie. When her husband came home late one evening he was welcomed by the sight of her sitting on the sofa, legs straddled, wearing nothing but her new undies and staring seductively into his eyes. He made for her and started passionately ripping off her bra and panties, but once he'd got them off he threw them on the ground, took out his penis and began pissing all over them. He then went upstairs to bed and left her there shivering and whimpering. This single act of urinating was more humiliating than all the years of abuse and when he awoke the next morning she was gone.

mouthwash

A friend of mine who used to hang around with a group of punks in his youth told me how he still feared for his life after maliciously pissing in one of their mouths.

They had all gone out camping in the forest one October night and were loading up on cider and drugs when my friend Ed decided to get some kip. Out of some warped need to assert his authority and justify his rank as the most intimidating of the bunch, one of the punks began puncturing Ed's tent with his penknife. Fearing a beating, Ed allowed the bully punk to continue unhindered until he had slashed the tent to shreds.

As Ed lay by the campfire and the rest were asleep in their tents he began feeling the cooling effects of alcohol and the injustice of his predicament. The powerful urge for revenge overcame him and when he saw his aggressor's head sticking out of one of the tents he felt the tide of bravery swell inside him and took out his dick and pissed, first, all over his hair, then his face, then finished off pissing into his assailant's wide-open unassuming mouth. In the morning Ed wasn't around but he heard that the bully punk saw the wet patch around his head and could smell piss in his hair.

Such a contemptuous action inspires violent reaction and had it not been for a joy-riding accident which rendered the bully punk immobile for four years, Ed believes he'd probably be dead by now.

pint pinchers Be paranoid

Did you ever wonder why there are so many half-full glasses of beer left around the tables at the end of a night? Exacerbated by the prevalence of drinks being stolen, some publicans have set up a vigilante group who will be stationed in every pub, club and watering hole in the country. On hearing that pints are being pinched, half-empty glasses of stout will be filled with piss so that they look like fine frothy pints of lager. Once cooled, the pints will then be placed in the most obtainable positions around the bar. So pint pinchers beware.

pale ale

My late grandfather told of a trick he tried to play on a man who used to get free pints by going from pub to pub tasting beers while blindfolded. This man would arrive at a pub and slam a fist full of coins on the counter and shout, 'Ten shillin's says I can tell the name of any beer just be tastin' it.' Beer at the time would have cost only a shilling so with the locals eager to win the price of ten more beers they would blindfold the man and ply him with pints until their money ran out.

One night he had the misfortune to enter the pub where my granda was drinking. The money was slammed down, the betting words said loud and the locals gathered round to get in on the fun. One by one the pints were sunk and this man was able to identify them all, from Perry's to Cherry's, to Mountjoy pale ale. With no more beer left in the house and no willing combatants left, the blindfolded man asks, 'Is dar no one left who tinks dey can beat me?'

My granda took a glass from the bar and at no loss to his own pocket filled it with piss and said, 'Aye, there's one more.'

Now, as there were no coolers or gas in those days, beer was served flat and at room temperature so handing him a warm glass would not have given the game away. The man took the glass and, not only the onlookers, but the entire pub fell silent fearing there might be a brawl.

They all gasped when he took the first gulp, but there was no reaction, he just tilted his head quizzically, and said nothing. He then took an even larger gulp, but still looked unsure. All the men had pained faces from holding their breath so long. He took one last sup and with his blindfold still on, he slammed the glass down on the counter, grabbed the money and said, 'Yis ain't foolin' me dis time lads, dat's piss!' With that the men in the pub fell about the place laughing. The barman gave the poor unfortunate a free pint to wash down the taste and cast a disparaging 'ye dirty ole bollix' look at my granda as he went about washing the glass.

The word 'loo' comes from Londoners who, upon pouring out the contents of their chamber pots on to the street would shout the warning 'Gardez l'eau'.

after dinner jokes

A PSYCHOLOGICAL PINT OF PISS

A man walks into a small London pub, orders a pint, sits down and drinks it. When the barman isn't looking, he stands up on his chair and, to the horror and amazement of the other customers, refills his glass with his piss without spilling a drop, pulls up his zip, and walks out.

The next day he comes in again, orders a pint from a different barman and drinks it at the same table. When he finishes, he stands up and again pisses a perfectly aimed pint.

On the third day he comes in at the same time, and although the locals warn the barman, he doesn't believe them until he sees the man half-way through the act. The barman rushes over and just as the performer is pulling up his fly, grabs him and throws him out and tells him never to come back again.

The next day, though, word has spread and before the pisser's normal time of arrival, the pub is crowded with new customers awaiting the spectacle. At 1.30 p.m. sharp he walks in the door, goes up to the bar and orders a pint of beer. The barman pauses, then makes a wise economic decision and

170

allows the pint piddler to carry out his stunt.

Months go by, the media have found out about it and the pub has become very popular with performers of all sorts of strange antics but the pint piddler remains the favourite amongst the rabble.

On the day of the pub's name change from the 'Peddler's Point' to the 'Piddler's Pint' the barman thinks, 'Right, this guy's great but he's got a problem.' The barman takes him aside and tells him that he'll continue to pay the price if he goes to a psychologist to get himself sorted out.

The pint piddler agrees and having been absent for three

weeks returns to the pub. He nods and waves to all those present – goes up to the bar asks for a pint and sits down. All eyes are on him as he sips his pint. He finishes his pint, stands up on the chair, takes out his mickey and to cheers and squeals, he refills his glass with deadly accuracy.

As he's leaving, the barman grabs him and, over the sound of the applause, shouts, 'I thought I sent you to a psychologist to get you sorted out?'

'You did and I went.'

'So what are you doing back here getting up to your old tricks?'

'Well,' answered the pint piddler before he closed the door behind him, 'at least now I know why I'm doing it.'

A month later a local goes up to the barman at the Piddler's Pint and bets him £300 that he can stand up on a bar stool and fill a pint glass full of piss. Knowing there was only one man in the bar who could do this, the barman reckons he's onto a sure bet and so agrees. The man hops up on the bar stool and takes out his dick and starts pissing. He misses the glass and pisses all over the counter.

The barman cracks up laughing at the man's efforts and tells him to hand over the money. He does this gladly and then sits down with his friends whereupon he starts laughing out loud. The barman calls him over and asks what's so funny. The man tells him, 'I bet my mates £600 that I could piss on the bar counter and not only would you say nothing but you'd also have a good laugh.'

OBSERVATION IS THE KEY

'Observation is the key to the practice of medicine', the ageing doctor told the on-looking students. From his old oak lecture table he raised up two full glass decanters which had been standing there since the beginning of the lecture. The colour of the liquid in them and the absence of his usual glass of water on the table seemed to corroborate the rumours of his urine-drinking habits, and caused whispers and sniggers to ricochet around the lecture room.

'If there had been a mix up,' he asked young Maurice, 'how could you tell which of these urine samples is that of a diabetic?' Seeing the blank look on his face, he glared intently around the room and announced dramatically, 'Sugar! One will be

sweeter than the other.' Then, to the disaffection and disgust of the students, he dipped his wrinkled finger into each decanter, brought it slowly up to his grinning mouth and sucked his finger to taste the difference.

'The absence of insulin,' he continued, as if he had done something as commonplace as coughing, 'in a diabetic's body means that they cannot naturally regulate their sugar intake, and so require a daily injection of pig's insulin to balance it out. The sweeter sample will be that of the diabetic. Now you are all going to try it for yourselves.'

He summoned all the students from their seats. Amidst the many 'ughs' and 'aghs' and philosophical 'to save another's life one must' musings, the students gathered round his oak table, and each in turn persuaded themselves to go through with it.

Once they had all tested the urine samples and returned to their seats, the doctor turned his back on them. Taking a stub of chalk out of his white surgeon's coat pocket, he wrote the words, 'Observation is the key to the practice of medicine', on the blackboard and underlined it.

He walked away from the blackboard to let the students jot down his words of wisdom. He bowed his head, took a small pause for thought, then reaching over his table and raising one of the decanters above his head, he pointed his withered left hand at the black board.

'Had you all observed me properly,' he said, with a terrible intensity, 'you would have noticed that I dipped my middle finger into each glass and sucked my forefinger.'

Úna Ryan is an Irish MEP who has the misfortune of being constantly referred to as Ms U. Ryan.

SHITTY SHOES AND PISSY TEA

A foreign journalist, writing an article on the rivalry between Catholic and Protestants in Scotland, stops a Celtic supporter before a match and offers him a free ticket to stand in the terraces with the Rangers fans. He also promises him £100 if he returns to tell him what happened. The Celtic fan agrees, takes the ticket and makes his way to the other side of the stadium.

Clad from head to toe in green and white stripes, he sustains boos and jeers as he makes his way through the crowd. Once in the terraces, he plonks himself slap bang in the middle of the Protestant sea of blue and white. For the first ten minutes nobody says anything to him, but after Celtic score the first goal a big man beside him threatens him, 'See you, that's gonna cost you.' Feeling suddenly afraid for his life the Celtic fan measures up to him and replies,

THE HOT POCKET SYNDROME

'Yea, what a ye gonna do about it?'

'Well, for a start you can take this money and bring back four cups of tea.'

Thinking this was his escape route, the Celtic supporter accepts the money but before he leaves one of the other men says, 'Hey, we can't be sure you'll come back so leave one of your shoes behind.'

He hobbles off, gets the tea and returns to the four men in the terraces. They give him his shoe back but as he's putting it back on he feels a warm gooey substance envelop his foot. Saying nothing he looks up at the men but they're just sipping their tea and smirking away to each other. Five minutes pass and then one of the Celtic players does an outrageous foul that causes a Rangers player to be taken off on a stretcher. One of the other burly men says to the Celtic supporter:

'That's gonna really cost you. Go buy another four cups of tea, this time with your own money.' The first man butts in and says, 'and leave your other shoe.' Duly he goes off again. When he arrives back he gives them the tea and puts his shoe back on, only this time there's little room for his foot what with the amount of fresh faeces inside. Again he says nothing, but stays quiet as half the terrace chortle to each other at his expense.

At half-time he meets up with the journalist who hands him the money and asks him about the behavioural dynamic of two sworn enemies. Taking the money he says, 'As long as they keep shitting in our shoes... we'll keep pissing in their tea.'

(Sung to the tune of the Latin hymn Gaudeamus Igitur)

Have you ever seen Mary pass water?
There's no stranger sight to be seen
As it flows for a mile and a quarter
You can't see Mary for steam.

Why do men flush the toilet before they're finished?

Listening to a comedy show once, I heard the performers in question list off their version of the seven wonders of the world. I remember two, the first being: 'Why do kamikaze pilots wear helmets?' and the seventh being: 'Why do men flush the toilet before they finish?' I knew the answer to this conundrum instantly, but I still wonder about the kamikazes...

You see, when I was younger I remember hearing my dad blasting away, full speed ahead, and suddenly, for no apparent reason, Whoosh! went the cascading sound of the flush overpowering the now engulfed and overwhelmed gush of his piss.

'Sacrilege!' thought I, 'how could someone ruin one of the most pleasurable moments of their piss?' That immense sense of achievement, the feeling that you are making some impact, and then to just go and spoil it like that? It's like the difference between throwing big rocks into a mass of gravel, and throwing pebbles at an avalanche. What kind of malicious parasite could embed itself in the brain causing one to deprive themselves of the pleasure and pride of a loud piss? This was an issue that I felt needed to be addressed.

My old man returned from doing his duty, but I didn't really know how to raise the question with him. Instead I vowed to my own shocked sensibilities never to do such a thing. But a few days later, whilst thrashing an old cigarette butt to pieces in the bowl, I found myself instinctively doing as he did. I heard my mind yell, 'Hey, hand, stop! I haven't finished yet.' But, alas, there was nothing I could do. My hand reached up, as if possessed by some evil force, and pulled the chain. The water came rushing down and ruined my pee. My only consolation was that my last few dribbles ended after the flushing had stopped. I walked out of the toilet that day feeling very annoyed that I had inherited such a brutal, self-inflicted irritation. But by God, how wrong I was, it is one of the most exciting skills a young man can master.

A few days later, as I was peeing away, practising my joined writing, my hand became possessed again. It reached up, pulled the chain and Whoosh! 'Ah, No!' I screamed, 'What a pisser!' Yet another spoilt piss. I summoned up my senses to adapt to the situation, to squeeze some sort of pleasure out of this travesty of a pee. But there were no dribbles. To my astonishment everything had stopped at the same time. Wham! It hit me like wet toilet paper in the face. What a breakthrough! I would most definitely have to try that again.

I ran downstairs, grabbed a pint glass and filled it up with water, swallowing the lot in one gulp, and waited anxiously for the urge. I was determined to prove to myself that this was not just a one-off, slash-in-the-pan event. The urge came without too much delay. I ran up to the jax, positioned myself and began to pee. Again my hand reached up instinctively and pulled the chain. As it flushed I kept peeing, never once interfering with its natural flow, and lo and behold, down to the cistern's last and my last drops they both simultaneously ceased to flow. What a revelation! Feeling though that perhaps it wasn't such a great feat, since I had grown up with that toilet and would have known how long the flush took subconsciously, I decided to try my newfound skill on as many different lavatories as possible. Each time the result was an outright success. Had I inherited an incredible and fulfilling skill?

the eighth wonder of the world

I thought of writing to that comedy show to suggest a new world wonder for them: Why do women enter the loo for two seconds, flush the toilet and walk back out again? But I found the answer to that one when I went in after one such speed-loo user. Wind.

If you want to cause a few laughs in a bar, ring them from your mobile and ask them to make an announcement over the PA for Ivanna Tinkle.

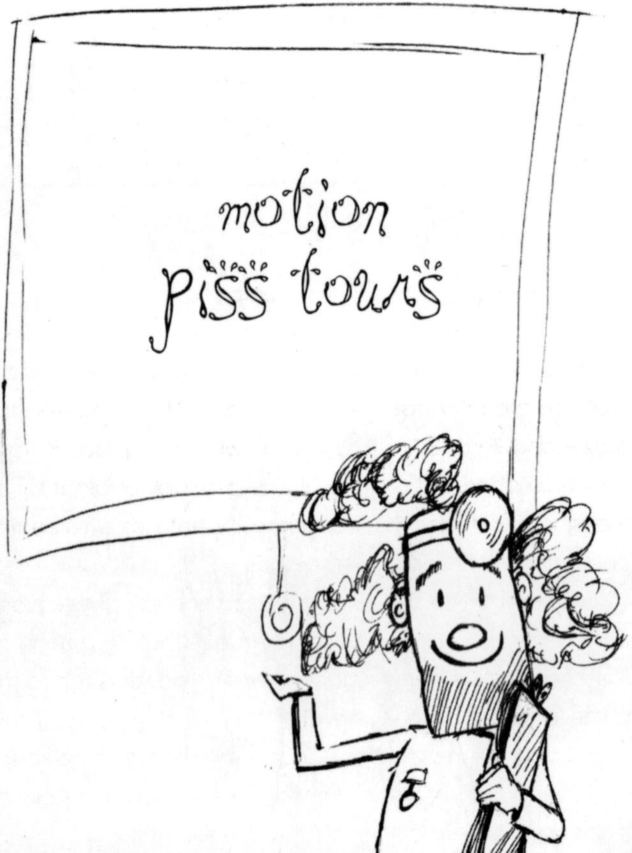
motion
piss tours

how to piss on the move

This section will deal with moments of motion when one must micturate: those times when pissing anywhere becomes a must because you feel your bladder will burst.

pissing off a rowing Boat

My brother was making his way out to the Blasket Islands one fine day. Having lolled his hand over the side of the small boat, he felt a dire need to be relieved. But his predicament on a punt made pissing a problem. He pondered the puzzle and figured that, no matter where he piddled from, he would capsize the boat. Noticing a lack of urgency on the islanders' faces, he wondered if centuries of breeding had rendered their bladders bigger.

He asked a well sea-fared islander, and no, genes didn't aid infrequency – they'd done the deed before getting on the boat. But successive generations of islanders faced the same problem, and eventually arrived at a solution that didn't involve capsizing the boat. He was told to go to the tip of the boat, rest his two knees on either side and point his penis up to project his piss out into the Atlantic.

In a community laden with sea-faring superstitions there were no *pisreóig* (superstitions) about this practice. Why he didn't just piss in the water-scooping canister, on board every small boat, and throw that out to sea, I don't know, but I do wonder what they might do when they need to pooh.

Pissing from a Van in traffic

I was in a minibus on the way to the airport, in heavy traffic and bad weather, with half an hour left before we were due to check in and an hour of travel left to go. The driver said there was no time for a piss stop. But a bursting bladder being the demanding bitch it is, I was forced to find some way to relieve myself.

I tried some cans and bottles but even among friends the fiend wouldn't flow. I considered pissing into my didgereedoo and sticking it out the window but I was teaching one of the others in the band. Suddenly a rush of adrenalin consumed my fears, I heard my mind say, 'wherever there's a willy, there's a window,' and before I knew it I found myself rammed up against the interior frame trying to figure out German sliding window mechanisms.

That conquered, I had to overcome another great task: how to keep my mickey dry, alive, and interested while the van sped along the motorway into full force wind, sleet and rain.

Well, of course I managed! Don't forget that I am the greatest piddler alive! Ignoring the outraged horn-honking from those overtaking, I cupped my mickey with my hand and pissed for about two or three miles.

pissing from the top of a Bus

In India bus journeys can take up to three days with few, if any, stops. Whilst travelling in the Himalayas one friend of mine remembers sitting on the roof of a bus with a few mates and the entire bus passengers' luggage. Their moonshine-swilling busman was driving through the night at breakneck speed, not slowing down for corners where the only space separating them and an oncoming car was the sheer drop off the cliff face. Being scared out of their wits so often, they were very close to pissing themselves. They didn't know it yet but sitting on the roof gave them a slight advantage over the squeeze below.

So what was she to do? Pissing off the side might see her hurled into the air at the next corner; pissing where she was sitting would soil her and her friends' clothes; and pissing on to the front window would further obscure the driver's view. So pissing off the back seemed the only option. She made her way to the back by climbing over the bags and boxes and then climbed down the ladder, hitched her skirt and held on for dear life.

When she began to piss she got a strange feeling that if she were to die on that bus journey she would have achieved a feat few, if any, had achieved before. Seeing that it was possible, her friends followed suit and when they all finished it was presumed that they left a ten-mile trail of urine on steep verges of that Himalayan pass.

comfort stop

Compare these figures:

Dublin to Dingle – 300 miles
– 7 hours (by bus)

Dublin to New York – 3,000 miles
– 7 hours (by plane)

Yes, it's true, in the time it takes you to travel from one side of Ireland to the other by bus you could have flown to America, Canada or Russia. For less than a bus ticket to the west, you could've flown to London, done some shopping, taken a photo of punks pissing in Trafalgar Square, had tea with the prime minister and made it back to Dublin in time for last pints.

Most touring companies take bloating bladders into consideration: aeroplanes drown you in piss-inducers like coffee, tea and beer; boats have an even bigger selection and trains do the same, but they all have toilets in which you can piss or puke it all back up. But bus companies in Ireland haven't caught on to the fact that most people travelling for more than two hours will need to empty their bladders.

I once heard a woman, who got on a four-hour bus journey from Limerick to Dublin, ask the driver if there was a going to be a loo stop. Well, you've never seen a man so shocked. He looked as if his mammy's morals and Christian speech etiquette had been mortally offended. He rose his nose in disgust, tightened his lips and with a smarmy brush of his seven strands of hair across his bald forehead answered with polished politeness, 'there will be a 15-minute comfort stop in the town of Borris-in-Ossory.'

She looked like she wanted to ask if she had time to go before the bus left, but couldn't bring herself to further offend the poor man.

But 'comfort stop'! Have you ever heard anything as ludicrous in your whole life? Of all the sanitised versions of what most of us, without any qualms, call a 'piss stop', this has got to take the prize for the most preposterous choice of words to avoid mentioning 'you know, ahem, eh, down there, Ahem!' Let's mount a bronze sculpted pooh on a slab of marble and present it to that prize pillock from Bus Éireann for being the saddest man in Ireland.

The driver was not exposing the fact that bus travel was an uncomfortable travel option, whose only consolation to passengers was the aforementioned 15-minute comfort stop. No, he was aggrieved by her use of slang. This colloquially-challenged man was quite definitely one of society's worst kind: prude and prissy, stiff and starchy, prim and priggish, straight-laced and stuffy. So the judge's decision is final, let's get on with the ceremony.

One of the many items the Japanese sell to mask toilet sounds is a loo roll holder with a built-in radio for home use.

during the filming of ryan's daughter ...

John Wayne was approached by a Kerryman returning from the toilet in the local tavern, the Kerryman pointed to his thigh and grinned saying, 'You left a patch of piss on your trousers'. To which John replied, 'You Irish have no manners, every time I'm taking a leak in this town the guy pissing next to me turns right around and says, "Jaysus! are you John Wayne?"'

laws regarding
pissing in public

irish ways and irish laws

A drunken twenty-one-year-old bloke, who was caught pissing on the pavement and making every effort to reveal his behaviour to passersby, was recently ordered by the prosecuting judge to write an apology on an A4 page and hold this page up for public viewing for three hours on Dublin city's main thoroughfare, O'Connell Street. I wonder did the dream definition below have any bearing on that judge's odd punishment.

 Dreaming that you are urinating in public symbolises lack of privacy in your affairs or signifies you need to make a public apology or confession.

Questions and answers

There is no precise law banning pissing in public in Ireland. Offenders instead will be prosecuted under the Public Order Act of 1994, which deems all sorts of behaviour offensive but only if there is someone in the vicinity to take offence.

I read up on it but I was still very unclear so I rang the garda press office and asked them to clarify some queries. I told the press officer that I'd heard mention of an seventeenth- or eighteenth-century by-law which stated that carriage drivers could legally piss against their own cartwheel if they pissed 'on the seventh spoke perpendicular to the pavement'. Would this old law allow today's taxi drivers to urinate on their own wheels?

He told me that all of those by-laws were made redundant by the 1994 public order act. He explained that if a woman and child were passing while the taxi man was watering his tyres they could take offence, so in fact pissing on the wheels could constitute a crime.

The same police press officer then told me that you wouldn't be arrested if were pissing out of sight down an alley because no one could take offence. When I asked him if a policewoman saw this person pissing down an alley could she be the one to take offence? He mentioned a court ruling that made him conclude that policewomen/men are not so easily offended.

PUBLIC ORDER ACT IRELAND

5.(1) It shall be an offence for any person in a public place to engage in offensive conduct

(a) between the hours of 12 o'clock midnight and 7 o'clock in the morning next following, or

(b) at any other time, after having been requested by a member of the garda síochána to desist.

(2) A person who is guilty of an offence under this section shall be liable on summary conviction to a fine not exceeding £500.

(3) In this section 'offensive conduct' means any unreasonable behaviour which, having regard to all the circumstances, is likely to cause serious offence or serious annoyance to any person who is, or might reasonably be expected to be, aware of such behaviour.

Upon being arrested state this defence:

My piss is clean, safe and medicinal, and I can list a thousand and one toxic chemical pollutants that you let into the atmosphere illegally to aid the destruction of the environment. For example, there should be a law against you driving that car because the acid rain caused from your exhaust fumes is killing the trees that produce the oxygen we all need to breath. So

if you don't mind, you servant of morally-muddled clowns, could you please arrest the true environmental offenders, and let me piss in peace?

must police preserve women's dignity?

Is it true, I asked him, that a policeman may not arrest a woman for defecating in public? Instead they had to preserve her decency by covering her from the gaze of the public. This leniency is lodged in the understanding that the urge to defecate could not be controlled as easily as the urge to urinate. The garda press officer told me that that was plainly untrue and quoted the case of a nineteen-year-old woman from Kildare who was given the probation act for crouching down in front of a garda squad car.

> Due to the ability of toilets in Japan to continuously flush, women would flush the toilet on average seven times per visit. This was costing so much money and causing such a shortage of water during the hotter months that hoteliers and other public centres installed touch button flush recordings.

dogs and horses

I then asked him if the owners of police dogs and horses who soil the pavement could be penalised by the law. No, he said, they have some arrangement with the varying councils across the land. But he had no answer when I asked whether a woman of a squeamish disposition could take offence and successfully prosecute upon witnessing police horses pissing and shitting on the streets.

worldwide fines

Long before there were paved streets there were dusty thoroughfares. Men and women evacuated fluids from their bowels happy in the knowledge that the earth would absorb them and the rain would wash them away. Back then few public representatives dared make human nature an offence. But as governments allow us to pollute the planet with chemical poisons they are now diverting our attention from the real threat by focusing their attention on the natural act of urinating. For some unknown reason, squeamishness and an abhorrence of the fruit of our bowels follows once natural landscapes have been turned into cities.

In America, the game is up for the public piddlers, as laws are being enacted in cities all over the country.

* In Walnut Creek they adopted a ban making pissing in public (PIP) a crime. It is punishable by up to six months in prison.

* In the city of Lincoln it is unlawful for any person to urinate or defecate on a public street, alley, or any other property, public or private, open to or visible to the public. Minimum $100 fine.

* Authorities in an Ohio city are charging people who urinate in public with littering because it's too difficult to get convictions for indecency and a conviction for littering carries a maximum of 60 days in prison and a $500 fine.

* A Chicago politician wants drunk baseball fans who urinate in public, of whom 30% are women, to get an automatic $340 fine, because public piddlers can only be arrested for disorderly conduct or public nudity which only carries a fine of $17.

* In Nova Scotia the fine for pissing in public is a strange figure of $157.50.

* In Africa the city fathers of Swaziland's third largest city, Siteki, have set up a posse of 'pee inspectors' to roam the streets and fine anyone found PIPing.

Even England has begun banning PIPing.

* In South Gloucestershire the offender may be fined a maximum of £500 in the magistrate's court.

* Police in Wrexham scour the streets after last orders armed with bleach, buckets and toilet brushes. They seize upon offenders and offer them a choice: either clean up the mess or face a fine. 99.9% are said to be cleaning up.

pee pods - the Best solution

In Holland the police very kindly make brochures available in all coffee shops, asking tourists not to piss in the streets because the uric acid is destroying the old buildings. They ask that tourists use the toilets in the coffee shops or if desired they were welcome to piss in the police stations.

Knowing that many of the punters would be too stoned to heed polite police notices, the council came up with a most ingenious solution to stop people pissing on the streets. They deployed Pee Pods outside most clubs and bars around the cities. They are free standing, oblong-shaped plastic containers with raised platforms and small holes in which to pee. They can be easily taken away and emptied, cause no offence to passersby, and don't attract the usual smattering of public toilet nuisances, i.e. smack heads and cottaging gay men.

Would that all governments follow the fair-minded example of the Dutch and place these pods around their city streets. Solutions can be found that don't turn people into criminals.

epilogue

Alas, it is time to get off the pot. You've been sitting there for far too long. But before I go, or you go again, I have one last thing to say.

Our squeamishness with excreted bodily fluids has influenced society's behaviour in how it deals with all kinds of waste. The sewage system is great but it has divorced us from the consequences of our effluent. We may think that flushing it out of sight gets rid of it but it only turns it into a greater problem – forty-two per cent of Ireland's ground water is polluted because of faulty septic tanks. Twenty per cent of the world's drinking water is being flushed down the toilet annually.

The same attitude that assumes piss is dirty has made urinating in the streets a crime. Yet, paradoxically, pissing in clean water is perfectly legal. We each soil up to 12,000 gallons of clean drinkable water a year. We must realise that it is not civilised to piss in one's own water source; it is plain silly. Even animals know not to do this. Using water to ferry our waste fluids from one location to another is beyond reason, especially as there are toilet systems designed that do not use any water at all.

No society can ever be civilised until it can deal with waste in a manner that isn't hazardous to itself. Change will only take place when we as a people get over this unreasonable squeamishness and find ways to deal with human effluent which won't impact negatively on our environment.

So, my fellow apisstelites, in the name of foreskin, glands and all holey bits... may you go 'n' piss.

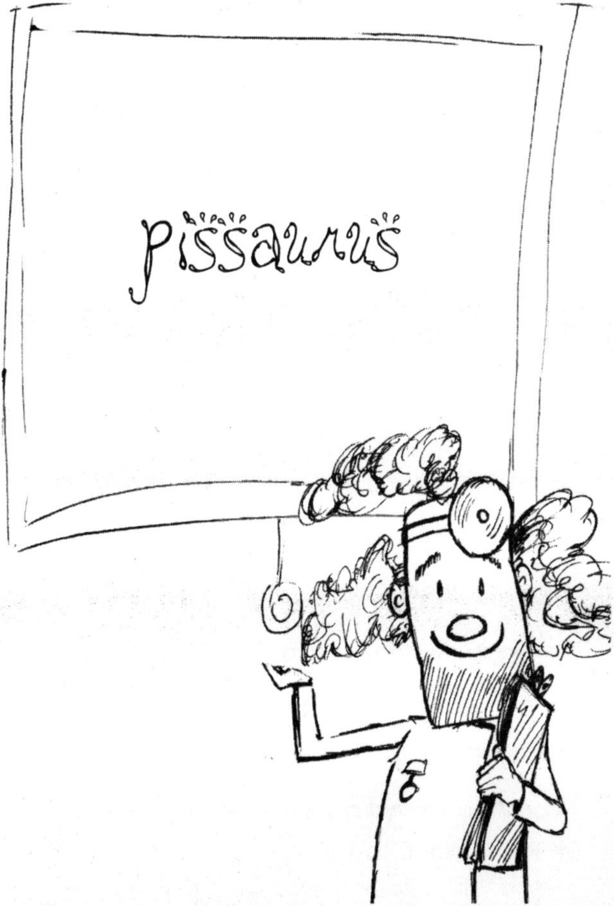
pissaurus

Some interesting employments of the word piss

* **Urinal:** Piss pot. Pissery or Pissoir (from French).

* **Go away:** Piss off. Go and piss up a shutter (1920s American).

* **Damn you:** Well, piss your fanny, you (Cork expression).

* **Insults:** You long streak of paralysed piss, you. Go piss up a rope, ya fuck stick. I spit on your corpse and piss on your grave (said with a Latin-American intonation).

* **Curse:** May you piss burning coals.

* **Angry:** Pissed (American slang).

* **Annoyed or unhappy:** I'm pissed off. He's well pissed off with you.

* **How annoying:** What a pisser. What a piss-off.

* **Negative exclamations:** Ah! Piss bombs! Ah! Piss balls! (meaning Damn It!).

* **Ants:** Pismires.

* **Sham elegance:** Piss-elegant.

* **Very unpleasant:** Piss awful.

* **Threatening phrases:** I'll rip your head off and piss down your neck. I'll pull out your eyes and piss on your brains. I'll kick your balls so far up your stomach you'll be pissing through your mouth. I'll spit on your corpse and piss on your grave.

* **Denoting velocity:** The thief went pissing around the corner and the police went pissing after him.

* **Philosophy of the depressed:** People are like pubes on porcelain, they eventually get pissed off. It's always better to be pissed off than pissed on.

* **Drunk:** Pissed, – as a fart, – as a Coot.

* **A drunkard:** A piss head. Pisso (Australian slang), piss artist, piss pot, piss tank.

* **Drinking heavily:** On the piss.

* **An occasion of heavy drinking:** A piss-up.

*   ***Any kind of alcohol:*** Piss (Australian).

*   ***Denoting incompetence:*** He couldn't organise a piss-up in brewery.

*   ***Denoting hatred:*** If you were on fire I wouldn't even piss on you.

*   ***Denoting meanness:*** He wouldn't give you the steam off his piss.

*   ***Denoting futility:*** You're all just pissing in the wind, pissing against the wind.

*   ***Mixing metaphors:*** You're pissing up the wrong tree.

*   ***Crap joke:*** What's the definition of revenge? A pole pissing on a dog.

*   ***Denoting weakness of flavour:*** That tea tastes like piss water. That's maidens' piss.

*   ***Denoting ugliness:*** He looks like a bulldog licking piss off a nettle.

*   ***Denoting uncontrolled laughter:*** I was pissing myself laughing.

* **Denoting fear:** I was pissing myself.

* **Dandelion tea and other diuretics:** Piss 'i' Bed.

* **Denoting worthlessness:** Pissant.

* **Denoting low position of employment:** Piss boy (a holder of buckets was employed so that civilised lords and ladies could relieve themselves without having to leave the dining table).

* **Labia minora and labia majora:** Piss flaps. Piss clam.

* **Messing around:** Pissing about.

* **Waste time, procrastinate:** Piss around, piss-farting around (Australian).

* **Let's stop wasting time:** Let's get outta here, we're just pissing for shits and giggles (Australian).

* **Bodily fluid lesson:** Why is piss yellow and sperm white? So men can tell whether they're coming or going!

* **Denoting poverty:** Piss poor.

* **Denoting inexpensiveness:** Piss cheap.

* **Denoting ease of execution:** Piss easy (opposite to shit hard).

* **Denoting lack of difficulty:** Piece of piss.

* **Denoting heavy menstruation:** Pissing blood.

* **It's raining heavily:** It's pissing down from the heavens.

* **It's going to rain heavily:** It's gonna piss.

* **To get very wet from rain:** I got pissed on.

* **Wet, drizzly, grey, damp and cold weather:** Pissy weather.

* **Denoting triumph:** We pissed all over them.

* **Denoting defeat:** We got pissed on.

* **Vagrant, waster, or one unaccomplished:** Piss artist.

* **Describing pain of cystitis or gonorrhoea:** Pissing razor blades, pissing broken glass.

* **Denoting a pause in travel for passenger relief:** Piss stop.

* **An appeal to those entrusted with a task not to purposely or inadvertently forget, fail or fuck up in any way:** Don't piss me about.

* **The morning erection:** My lad was piss proud (morning erections tend to be coupled with a full bladder).

* **Making a mockery or taking advantage of someone:** Taking the piss, pulling the piss.

* **A scripted mockery:** A piss take.

* **One who mocks:** A piss taker.

* **An encouraging phrase to make a decision:** Piss or get off the pot.

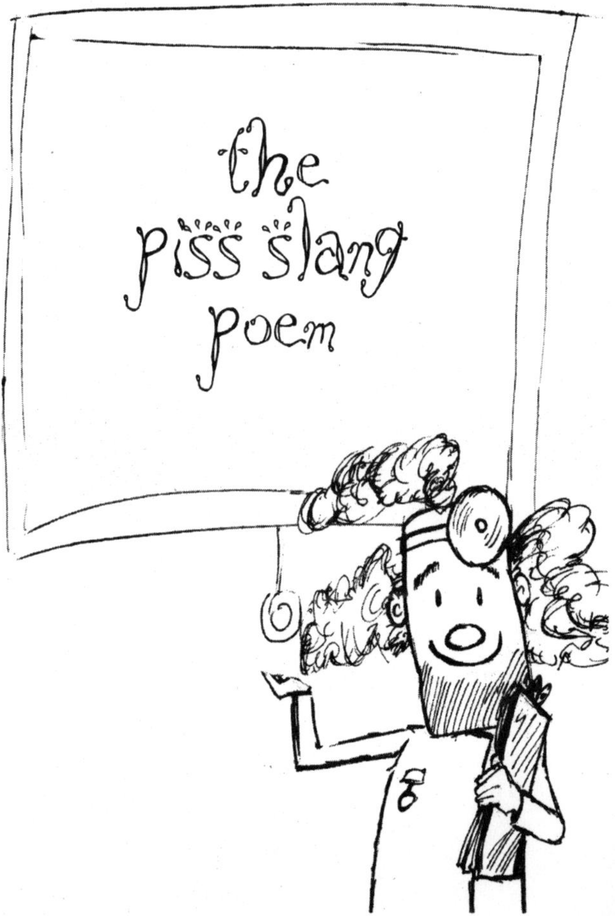
the piss slang poem

A GYPSY'S KISS

Siphon the python

Number one

Point percy at the porcelain

Checking the plumbing

Easing the springs

My back teeth are floating

Wet the whistle

Bleed the lizard

Let Niagara fall

Water the lawn, plants or flowers

Slash

Tinkle

Piss

Powder me prick

Golden shower

Lime

Cut 'n' dash

Empty the bag

Drain the spuds

Wizz

Wazz

Poolie
Piddle
Widdle
Jimmy Riddle
Wee Wee
Pee Pee
Spend a penny
Micturate
Urinate
Irrigate me mate
Drain the main vein
Pass water
Jaysus I'm bleedin burstin'
Drain the radiator
Lift a leg
Go play in the sand box
Ring out the monster
Let fly
Drain the dew from the lily
Go to the john
Go to the can
Make a pit stop

Drain the dragon

Pump ship

See a man about a dog

Take a leak

Take a whizz

Go for a gypsy's kiss

Relieve one's self,

Empty the bladder

Answer natures call

Excuse me while I powder my nose

I need to wet my whiskers.

By Professor J. Riddle

questionnaire

How do you hold your willy?

a With great difficulty ☐

b With the aid of a microscope ☐

c Like a true master ☐

Do you wipe the seat after spraying?

a What seat? ☐

b No, that's a woman's job ☐

c I lift it first ☐

How high can you piss?

a Higher than any man ☐

b When I'm as high as a kite ☐

c Accuracy is more important ☐

Have you ever pissed into a bottle?

a Yes, but it splashed all over me ☐

b I have and I'm a girl ☐

c I did but an elephant swiped it and gulped down the contents ☐

Have you ever made someone piss?

a Yes, by frightening them ☐

b Yes, by tickling them ☐

c Yes, because I am in fact a beer ☐

Can your mother pee whilst standing?

a That is her own business ☐

b I don't know, I'll ask her ☐

c I'm a horse, so, yes ☐

If you are a woman, would you use a urinal?

a I use them every day to practise my domestic skills ☐

b If our African village ever get them, then perhaps ☐

c If you are a woman then miracles do happen ☐

What did Max Liebermann say?

a I could sculpt his face out of snow ☐

b I could piss the old boy in snow ☐

c I pissed on his face as he lay in the snow ☐

How painful is acute cystitis?

a Like pissing razor blades ☐

b Like pissing burning coals ☐

c Like pissing malicious ants with strimmers ☐

Who is the greatest pisser of all time?

a   Professor J. Riddle ☐

b   Prof. Jimmy Riddle ☐

c   Professor J. R. ☐

Where is the College of Pissology?

a   Wherever two or more pissers gather ☐

b   Dáil Éireann ☐

c   Borris in Ossary ☐

Which pissing contest would you like to take part in?

a   The longest piss ☐

b   The furthest piss ☐

c   The drinking of piss ☐

Would you shake hands with your date if you hadn't cleaned your hands?

a I always clean my hands, how dare you! ☐

b Yes ☐

c Considering what we'd be getting up to it wouldn't be a cause for concern ☐

If you had to piss on the pitch would you:

a Wait till half time? ☐

b Wait till the ref wasn't looking? ☐

c Piss on the nearest player? ☐

How long can you hold your piss after starting?

a I can't, I'm useless ☐

b 30 seconds ☐

c Until I need to go again ☐

If you were to indulge in water sports would you:

a   Wear a swimming cap?   ☐

b   Wear a condom?   ☐

c   Wear down the carpet?   ☐

How do you deal with the last dribble?

a   Put toilet paper in my pants   ☐

b   Bring a spoon with me to the toilet   ☐

c   Use Riddle Inc. willy wipes   ☐

When you miss the pot do you:

a   Hope it soaks into the carpet?   ☐

b   Pour Domestos all over the carpet?   ☐

c   Pour salt and hope it soaks up like wine?   ☐

Can you piss with people beside you?

a   Only when I'm drunk ☐

b   Only when people are beside me ☐

c   Only when they are wielding whips ☐

Do you mix the urine you're about to drink with:

a   Warm tea? ☐

b   Orange juice? ☐

c   Someone else's? ☐

Did a daily urine facial help Jack Dempsey become world champion?

a   My father never did such a thing ☐

b   He wasn't a real man - boxing is all about the bruises ☐

c   Yes ☐

How many times do I have to tell you not to play in the cat litter?

a   Fifty times   ☐

b   Sixty times   ☐

c   Til I've gone blind   ☐

What is the funniest colour your piss has ever been?

a   Pale white   ☐

b   Red   ☐

c   Luminous green   ☐

If I told you it's a piece of piss being on the piss what with piss being piss cheap, would you think I was:

a   Pissed as a newt?   ☐

b   Pissed as a coot?   ☐

c   Pissed as a fart?   ☐

How do you say I need to do a liquid bladder movement?

a   Ich mus in dem toileten gehen   ☐

b   Caithfidh mé mo mhún
a scaoileadh   ☐

c   je dois faire un pee pee   ☐

What would you do if you saw a policeman pissing from a horse?

a   I'd report him immediately   ☐

b   I'd throw horse faeces at him   ☐

c   I'd start pissing up against the horse   ☐

If mostly A: WELL DONE
If mostly B: WASH YOUR HANDS
If mostly C: YOU DIDN'T BUY THIS TO READ IT